GUTIERREZ

Notes from a
Naturalist's Sketchbook

Notes from a
Naturalist's Sketchbook

◆————————————————————◆

by

CLARE WALKER LESLIE

Boston

HOUGHTON MIFFLIN COMPANY

1981

For their careful verification of the natural history information, I wish to give special thanks to Philip J. Darlington, Professor Emeritus of zoology at Harvard University; his wife, Elizabeth K. Darlington; and, Christopher W. Leahy, naturalist for the Massachusetts Audubon Society.

Library of Congress Cataloging in Publication Data

Leslie, Clare Walker.
  Notes from a naturalist's sketchbook.

  1. Natural history—Vermont—Pictorial works.
2. Natural history—Massachusetts—Cambridge—
Pictorial works. I. Title.
QH105.V7L47   574.9743   81-4064
ISBN 0-395-31298-1 (pbk.)   AACR2

Printed in the United States of America

B 10 9 8 7 6 5 4 3 2 1

For some years, I have been watching nature and keeping a field journal, following the seasons and noting the subtle changes that occur throughout each year. Since my husband and I have a home in Vermont and an apartment in Cambridge, Massachusetts, most of my observations are done in or near these two places. I have found that, rather than going to distant or more spectacular areas, I can see much happening in nature not far from my own doorstep.

When I was invited to publish my journals, I hesitated. What had I observed that was so unique or of special interest to the public? Besides, my journals are mine; they are private. They represent my own interest in observing and recording; no one else's. On the other hand, because the world of nature holds deep significance to me, I wanted to share with others what I have found so magical, complex, humorous, tragic, and magnificent in the natural world. And yes, we are all inextricably bound together. Destroy nature and we destroy ourselves.

The pages that follow were selected from my journals and have been redrawn to work into a more cohesive and reproducible format. Therefore, they do not represent one specific year but a compilation of all four years. The dates of particular pages correspond generally to the dates recorded in all my journals.

I ask those of you who read these pages to go into your own landscape. Find in it your own starlings, crocuses, house flies, or deer mice to observe. You need no fancy drawing skills to sketch chickadees at your feeder or milkweed growing in your back yard, or merely to jot down the daily changes in the weather.

If this journal inspires you to keep your own, or simply helps increase your awareness that things natural <u>do</u> live beside you, then I will realize it was right to share my observations publicly.

Vermont —

February, 1981

The new year does
not celebrate a
beginning but a
continuation of
life's processes.

Sunrise : 7:20 a.m.
Sunset : 4:15 p.m.

Days are already
three minutes longer.

Winter neighbors:

Red
squirrel
snatches
fallen
birdseed.

We hear pileated woodpeckers
more than we see them.

A porcupine
winters under
the barn.

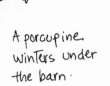

We run
a mouse
hotel.

January 3 - Vermont
2:30 p.m.
12° F and overcast

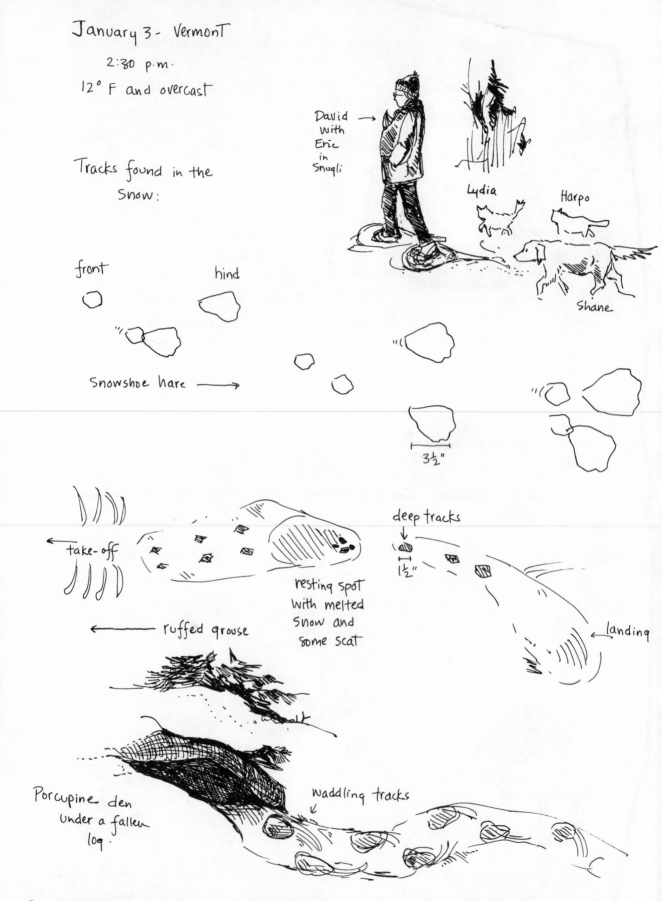

David with Eric in Snugli

Lydia

Harpo

Shane

Tracks found in the snow:

front

hind

Snowshoe hare →

3½"

deep tracks

1½"

take-off

ruffed grouse ←

resting spot with melted snow and some scat

landing

Porcupine den under a fallen log.

Waddling tracks

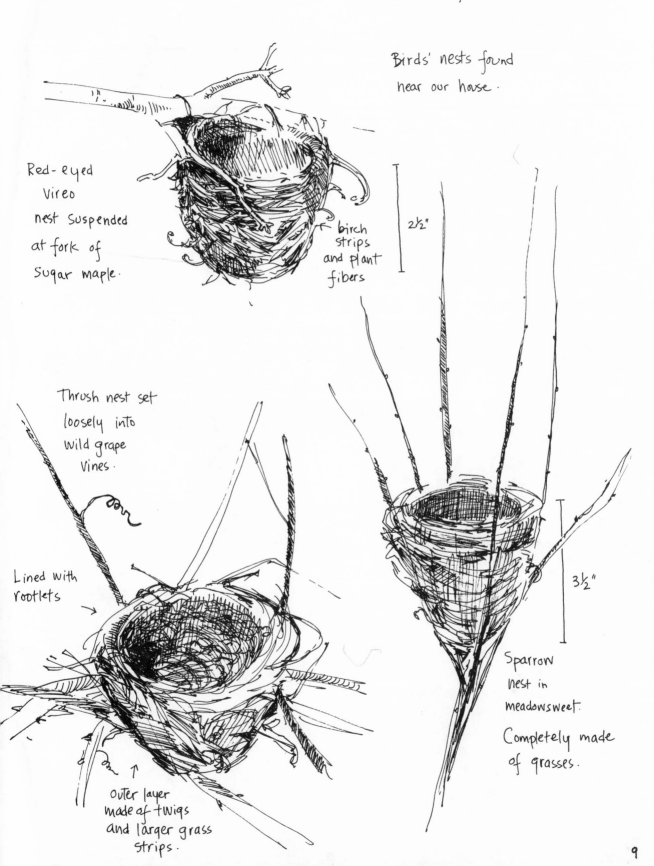

January 4 – Vermont

Birds' nests found
near our house.

Red-eyed
Vireo
nest suspended
at fork of
sugar maple.

birch
strips
and plant
fibers

2½"

Thrush nest set
loosely into
wild grape
vines.

Lined with
rootlets

Outer layer
made of twigs
and larger grass
strips.

Sparrow
nest in
meadowsweet.

Completely made
of grasses.

3½"

January 14 - Cambridge

23°F , raw and overcast

Back to the city after two
weeks of living closely
beside nature. Here,
nature appears only in
bits and pieces. But,
when discovered, sometimes
seems all the more
significant than when
it's there all
the time.

" peter-peter-
peter "

A titmouse
has been singing
in the silver
maple across the
street.

There is a coming brightness
to the daylight.

Bought some
crocus bulbs
in Harvard
Square.

January 24

January 15

January 23

One lusty
purple bud
and more
coming.

January 27

It's spring
on our
Window
sill.

January 16 — Cambridge

Mount Auburn Cemetery

1:50 p.m. low 40's
and sunny

remains of
snow

Distant
drone of traffic.
Otherwise,
wonderfully
quiet.

Slate-colored juncos
feeding on seeds in
shrubbery.

← red
tinged

Lilac buds
showing
some
green.

green
inner
bark

Bright emerald
leaves inside buds,
just waiting!

With Eric sleeping in
the Snugli, I lean up
against a tombstone
and feel a bit of the
sun's warmth on us
that would not have
felt as strong had
it been December.

January 20 – Vermont

When we arrived late last
night, outside temperature
was −14°F and
indoors was 5°F!
Silence so thick,
cut only by creaking
of branches and
one distant
owl hoot.

mouse holes

Winter mushrooms
found:

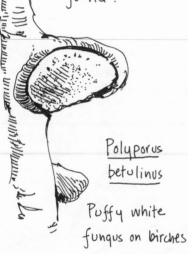

Mice even found
the peas I had put
in Eric's bean-
bag frog!

**Polyporus
betulinus**

Puffy white
fungus on birches

**Ganoderma
applanatum**
(artist's fungus)

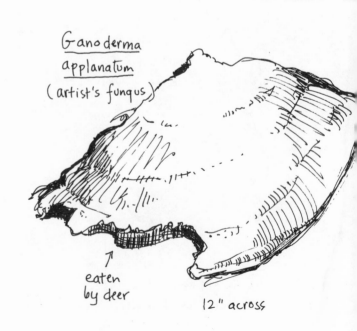

↑
eaten
by deer

12" across

Polyporus versicolor
(turkey tails)

Bands of
gray and brown on
a velvety surface.

Gall deformities found on various plants:

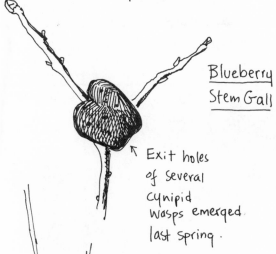

Blueberry Stem Gall

↑ Exit holes of several cynipid wasps emerged last spring.

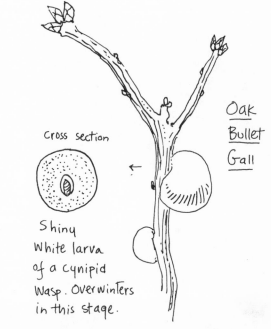

Oak Bullet Gall

cross section

Shiny white larva of a cynipid wasp. Overwinters in this stage.

Goldenrod Ball Gall

formed by a small fly

← chewed-out exit holes made by mice or woodpeckers getting at larva within

Cross Section

Elliptical Goldenrod Gall

← pupal skin shed in late summer by moth of gall-maker larva

Willow Shrub Pine Cone Gall

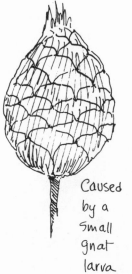

Caused by a small gnat larva

January 29—

McLean Hospital's land,
  Belmont

2:20 p.m.

mid 30°s and overcast

No longer snow
on the ground

A meadow edge

  in Winter

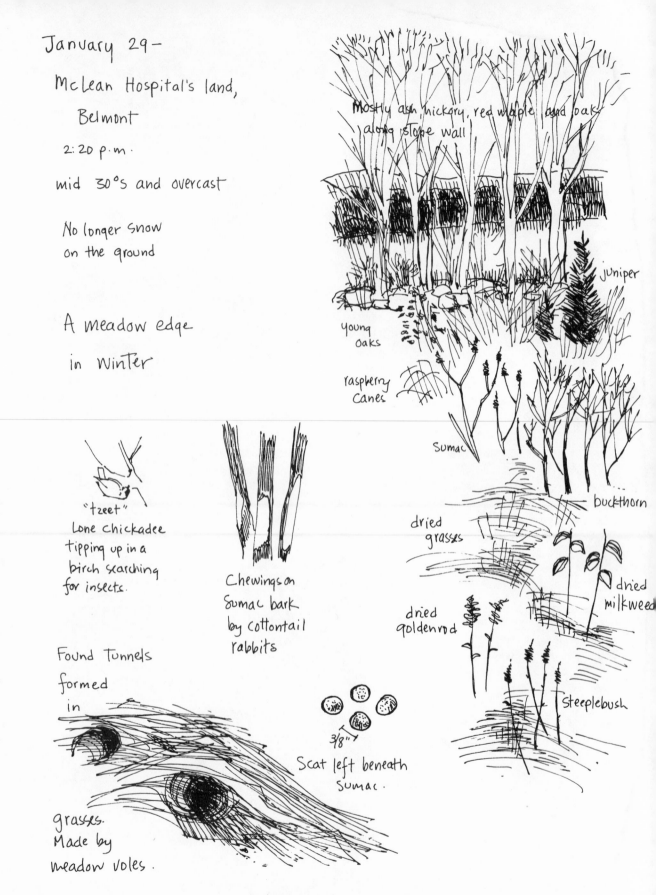

Mostly ash, hickory, red maple, and oak
  along slope wall

juniper

young
oaks

raspberry
canes

Sumac

"tzeet"
Lone chickadee
tipping up in a
birch searching
for insects.

Chewings on
Sumac bark
by cottontail
rabbits

dried
grasses

buckthorn

dried
goldenrod

dried
milkweed

Steeplebush

Found Tunnels
formed
in

3/8"

Scat left beneath
  Sumac.

grasses.
Made by
meadow voles.

much
tail shaking

Sunrise: 6:52 a.m.
Sunset: 5:05 p.m.

10:30 a.m.
From our window, watched
two gray squirrels
chasing each other over
our neighbor's roof.
Were they courting?

Chippewa name
for squirrel is
"ah-ji-duh-mo"
(tail in the air)

Chasing, courting, and mating
begins end of January. Young
are born in early March.

February 12 – Cambridge

  2:15 p.m.   33°F

Sunny with clear
  blue sky

Snowed yesterday.
Mostly melted today

Lots of chirping of
house sparrows and
chattering of starlings
in shrubs.

Noticed on a
Winter jog:

♂ mottled
red and
brown

♀ dull
brown

Male house finches
singing. Courtship
has begun. These birds
have recently become
common residents
in Cambridge.

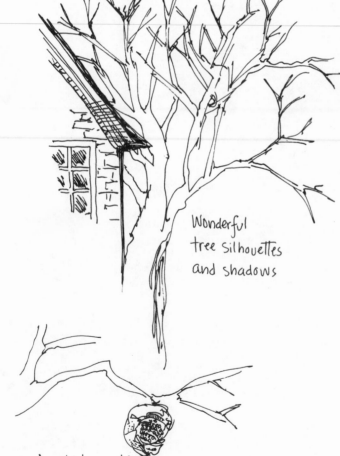

Wonderful
tree silhouettes
and shadows

An old hornet nest
hanging in tree branch over
Linnaean Street.

Gulls silently
passing over
roofs

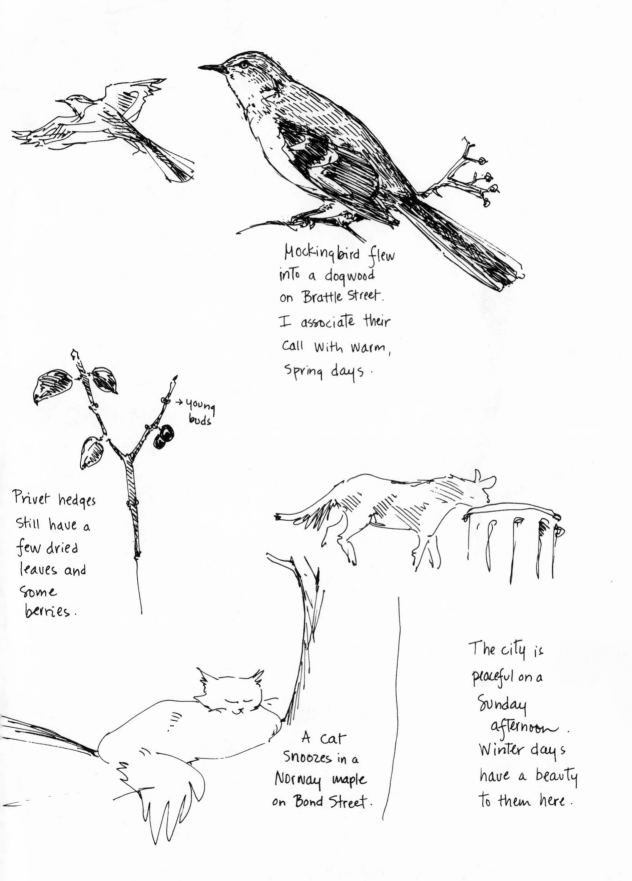

Mockingbird flew
into a dogwood
on Brattle Street.
I associate their
call with warm,
spring days.

→ young
buds

Privet hedges
still have a
few dried
leaves and
some
berries.

A cat
snoozes in a
Norway maple
on Bond Street.

The city is
peaceful on a
Sunday
afternoon.
Winter days
have a beauty
to them here.

February 17 - Vermont

Twigs from trees along
our road.

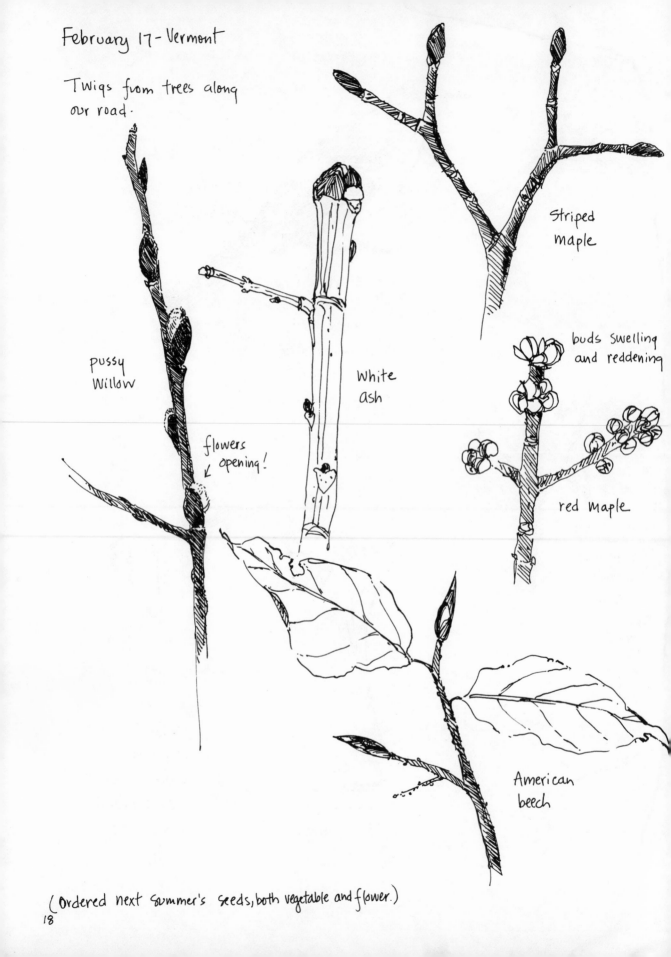

pussy
Willow

Striped
maple

buds swelling
and reddening

White
ash

flowers
opening!

red maple

American
beech

(Ordered next summer's seeds, both vegetable and flower.)

The birds that winter here often travel in small flocks - perhaps an advantage in warning of predators and finding scarce food.

1:20 p.m.

Winter storm watch broadcast on the radio. Beginning to snow heavily. Birds flock to the feeders.

evening grosbeaks

Lydia watches, hidden by a snow bank.

February 27 - Vermont

28° F

Three feet of
Snow on the
ground now.

Shane discovered
what seemed to be
a dead chipmunk
on the snowy road.

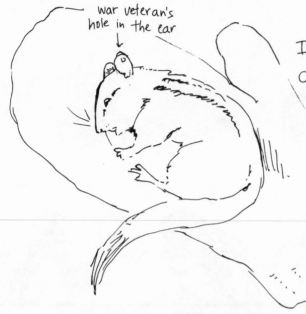

war veteran's
hole in the ear

I curled it in my mitten and
continued down the road. But after
a while, it seemed the body
moved. It struggled into a
smaller ball in my hand and
was, in fact, still alive!

What had brought it
into the road? Why
the lifeless state?
What should I do?

Then I noticed the
upper and lower
teeth had grown
together, forcing
the jaws open.
The creature was
starving and was
extremely thin.

Dark, yellowed
teeth. Sign
of an aging
animal?

I took it to a neighbor.
We tried coaxing some
milk into it and even
attempted cutting the
teeth to close the
jaw once more.

The shock of the cutting momentarily stirred it awake. But, could it survive? We decided to return the chipmunk to the spot where it had been found, hoping that natural events would find a better solution for its condition than we could.

I found a pocket of open ground in a snow bank along the roadside where we had found it. It curled into a tight ball as I piled snow up to form a warm cave.

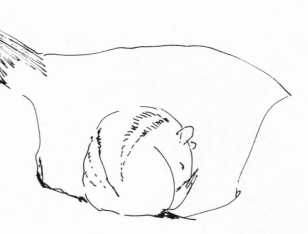

Would it revive? Would its jaws close? Was it too weakened to survive? Had I done the best thing by not interfering?

February 28 -
   David and I returned to look for the chipmunk. There it lay, curled in a different position, sleeping —

      Cold and still.

March 3 - Cambridge

6:30 a.m. Awakened by a "whoit-whoit-whoit-cheer-cheer" coming from somewhere outdoors. Opened the curtains to see a brilliant red male cardinal singing in the early morning sunlight.

Skunk tracks in the mud around a neighbor's trash can.

$1\frac{1}{2}"$

Daffodil and crocus leaves cutting through dirty remains of snow.

Willow buds turning yellow and swelling

Red epaulets exposed, wing and tail spread when sings.

"ok - a - leee"

Male red-winged blackbirds return before females, to choose nesting territories. Much singing and posturing occurs in defense of sites.

Some say spring arrives when the first red wings return.

For the last two years, at about the same time, a house sparrow pair begins actively courting outside my studio window.

Female flies in and out of hole in eaves of neighbors' house.

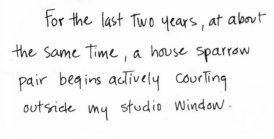

Male repeatedly mounts.

Female flutters wings to show receptivity.

House sparrows are known to court and mate for lengthy periods. Have observed this activity occurring from February until mid-May, even after young are born. (House sparrows can have several broods.)

Distinct "cheep-cheep" of male as he sits on fire escape.

an early bee

Tulip leaves coming up

March 18 -

<u>First</u> crocuses in bloom in a sunny, warm spot in front of the Christian Science Church near Mass. Ave.

March 19 – Vermont

30 - 32°F – blustery, menacing clouds

Air so fresh after Cambridge

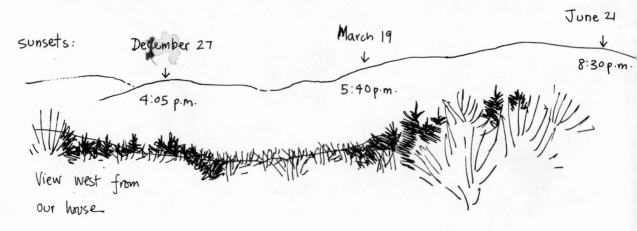

sunsets:

December 27
↓
4:05 p.m.

March 19
↓
5:40 p.m.

June 21
↓
8:30 p.m.

View west from our house.

Spring will arrive officially at 6:43 p.m. tomorrow evening.
When the sun sets, day and night will have an equal number of hours.
        Days are more brilliant and there's a whiff of Spring in the air
even with Ten inches of wet snow still on the ground.

Slate-colored

⅛"

A wingless, primitive insect living in leaf litter and moist areas. Moves by springing a forked tail from underneath its body.

" Snow fleas," not true fleas but a species of Springtail (order Collembola), appear across the snow like hundreds of black specks. They seem to appear during these last days of winter when there are patches of melting snow and rivulets of running water.

March 20 - McLean Hospital's
land, Belmont
6:30 p.m.
low 50's and mild

just dusk

Lay in the cool, dried
grasses listening to the nasal
"beezp-beezp" of a male woodcock
somewhere nearby.
Then, as dusk came fully on,
it rose and began spiralling
high into the sky in its
courtship flight.

Can rise to as
much as 200 feet
before it descends

after hovering
a few moments,
drops quickly
to the ground

fast ascent
with wings creating
a whistling sound

may repeat this
numerous times
during the evening
and for many
days

In late
March, males can be
seen at dusk doing this
elaborate flight pattern
in areas of wet thickets
or brushy meadows.

American Woodcock

Size =
11"

mottled
brown;
short wings,
long bill to
probe ground
primarily for earthworms.

March 31 - McLean Hospital's land,
               Belmont

10:20 a.m.

high 40°s

beautiful, late winter day
sunny and balmy

everything still wintry looking
from a distance

Sounds:

Cardinal = "wheet- wheet · wheet"
titmouse = "peter - peter - peter"
three crows = "caw- caw- caw"
traffic of Route 2

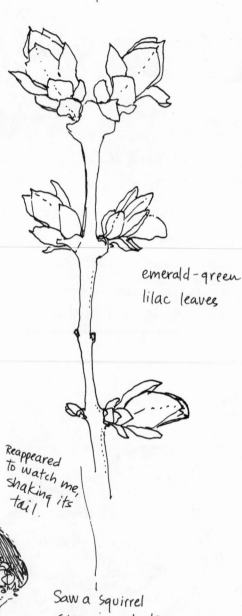

emerald-green
lilac leaves

but:

red
maples
in full
flower

♂
staminate
flowers

(♀ and ♂
flowers grow
in different
clumps on either
same tree or even
separate trees.)

x2

♀
pistillate
flowers

Reappeared
to watch me,
shaking its
tail.

Sat in the sun
drawing and for
the first time
did not get
chilled.

Saw a squirrel
carrying oak leaves
into a hole.
Male or female?
Beginning a nest?

Snowdrops outside
the apartment

Spattered by today's
rain and wiggling with
each breeze, they stand
like little ghosts under
the streetlight.

April 14 - Vermont

What contrasts there are
between Cambridge and Vermont:

Spring to winter
noise to quiet
closed spaces to open spaces
Suburban habitats to
   country habitats
no other people
   in sight

yellow →
brown →

Saw first butterfly
of the season, a
mourning cloak.
(It overwinters as
an adult in bark
crevices and under
house shingles.)

Red maples
just beginning
to show
some
flowers.
Spring here
is two
weeks
behind
Cambridge.

deep red
♀ flower
heads →

Leaves
nibbled
by insect
or mouse?

pale
violet →

Hepatica

Earliest wildflowers
coming up
in the woods.

Flushed a woodcock
in marshy spot behind
our house.

My bulbs are coming up!
early Tulips and crocuses

April 15 - Vermont

Sugaring-off at
Stanley Hubbard's
sugar house

Red Squirrels nibble
buds to get sap.

More than 1800 sugar maples
tapped from late March
until mid April

Sap poured into
house here

Takes 40 gallons of sap to
make one gallon of syrup.
Takes 4 maples, at least 40
years old, to yield enough sap
in 6 weeks to produce
1 gallon of syrup.

Thirty to thirty-five cords of
wood used each year to make
500 - 600 gallons of syrup.
Need 30° F. temperatures
during the day and 15-20° F
at night for a decent flow
in trees.

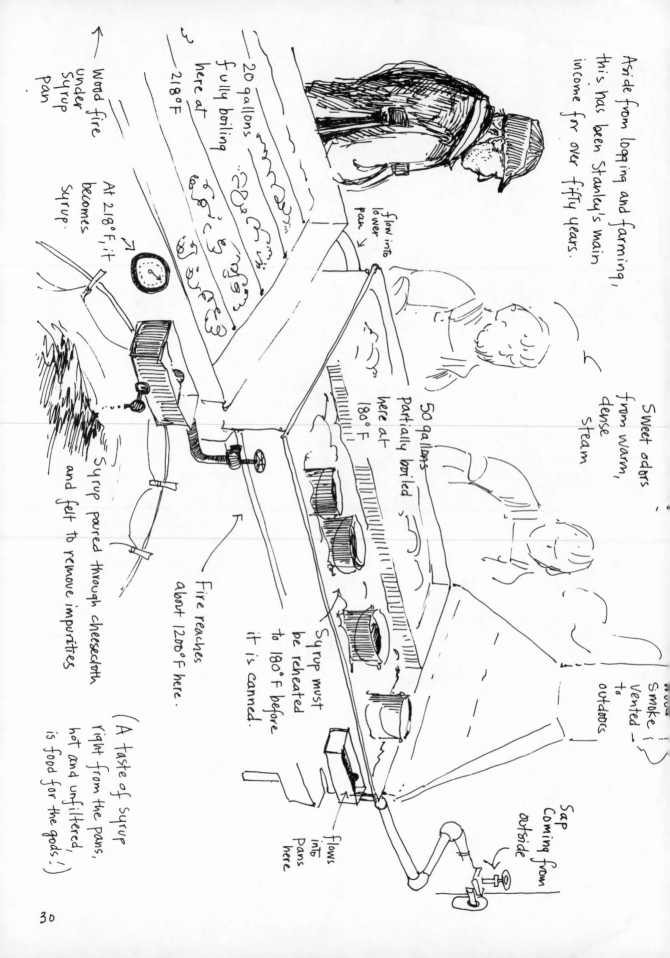

Aside from logging and farming, this has been Stanley's main income for over fifty years.

Sweet odors from warm, dense steam

Wood smoke vented to outdoors

Sap coming from outside

flow into lower pan

50 gallons partially boiled here at 180°F

Syrup must be reheated to 180°F before it is canned.

flows into pans here

(A taste of syrup right from the pans, hot and unfiltered, is food for the gods!)

20 gallons fully boiling here at 218°F

Fire reaches about 1200°F here.

Syrup poured through cheesecloth and felt to remove impurities.

At 218°F, it becomes syrup.

Wood fire under Syrup pan

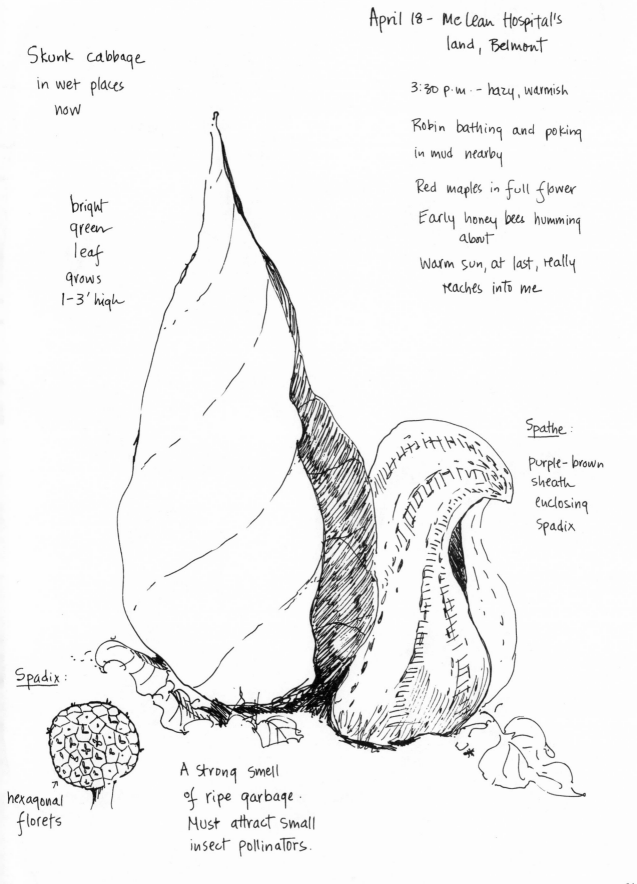

Skunk cabbage
in wet places
now

bright
green
leaf
grows
1-3' high

April 18 - McLean Hospital's
land, Belmont

3:30 p.m. - hazy, warmish

Robin bathing and poking
in mud nearby

Red maples in full flower

Early honey bees humming
about

Warm sun, at last, really
reaches into me

Spathe:

purple-brown
sheath
enclosing
Spadix

Spadix:

hexagonal
florets

A strong smell
of ripe garbage.
Must attract small
insect pollinators.

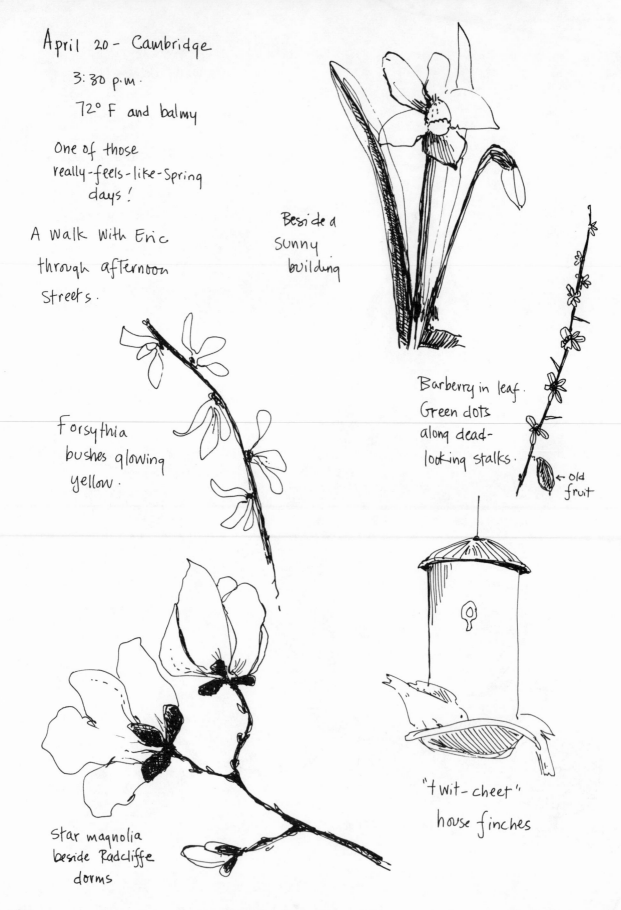

April 20 - Cambridge

3:30 p.m.

72° F and balmy

One of those
really-feels-like-Spring
days!

A Walk With Eric
through afternoon
streets.

Beside a
sunny
building

Forsythia
bushes glowing
yellow.

Barberry in leaf.
Green dots
along dead-
looking stalks.

← Old
fruit

Star magnolia
beside Radcliffe
dorms

"twit-cheet"
house finches

From an
old seed
Comes a
new maple

flew
past

E. watches
over my shoulder

ONE WAY

just
dropped onto
My page

⅛"

Yew shrubs
have little, yellow flowers

Norway
maple

ash

Silver
maple

flowers Coming out.

Beautiful unfolding
of origami-wrapped
forsythia leaves.

Robin chortles
in a cherry tree.

April 29 – Cambridge

Raining, an indoors day

Wet days help speed along
the greening of trees
and lawns.

I sit at my desk, with
binoculars, watching
a house sparrow
pair next door.

1.]

Male hops restlessly about
in Norway maple.

2.]

Finally alights
on roof and
peers into hole.

Has something in
its bill – insect?

Birds don't seem
to mind the wet.
Keep this up all day.
What commitment!

3.]

♂ in

♀ out

rain drops

They seem to communicate
Switch by much "chitting."

5.]
♂ returns
to roof above.
Twists head
constantly
keeping on
the alert.

"chit. chit"

ⓑ ♂ leaves
as ♀ returns

4.]

ⓐ ♀ appears in 15 minutes
with food in her bill.

(Must have young within hole.)

Still a tinge of winter here although dusk comes noticeably later and the air has a bit of warmth to it.

7:30 p.m. - Gertie's Pond

Everywhere sounds of water running
Red-winged blackbirds are back
Grasses showing bits of green
Some snow still in the woods
Daylight Saving Time makes for longer daylight

Peeps by passing air through inflated vocal sac in throat

³/₄"

Shined a flashlight on a peeper treefrog actually peeping.

Wood frogs and American toads croaking and trilling in beaver marsh.

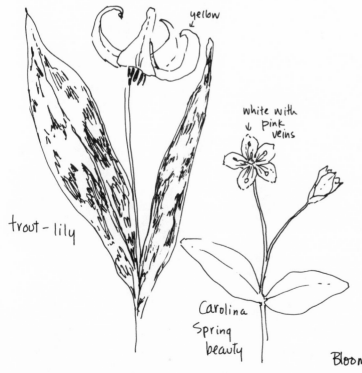

trout-lily

yellow

white with pink veins

Carolina Spring beauty

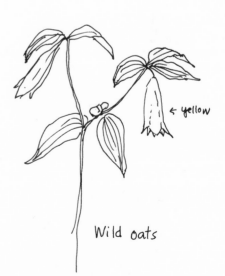

← yellow

Wild oats

Blooming in the woods.

May 6 – McLean Hospital's land,
Belmont

2:30 p.m.   mid 50°s

Raining solid for two days
Went to the woods to see
what was there in the rain.

Saw a pair of
wet starlings
in Cambridge
as I got into
the car.

← Eric in Snugli

Hope no one
sees me
here drawing
rain drops!

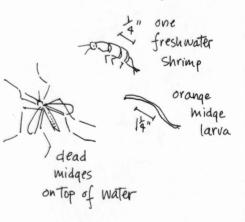

One went
into tree
hole by
our apartment.

A nest?

Scooped up water from
a temporary pond and found:

¼" one
freshwater
shrimp

orange
midge
larva
⅛"

dead
midges
on top of water

A sedge which
blooms early –
Carex pennsylvanica

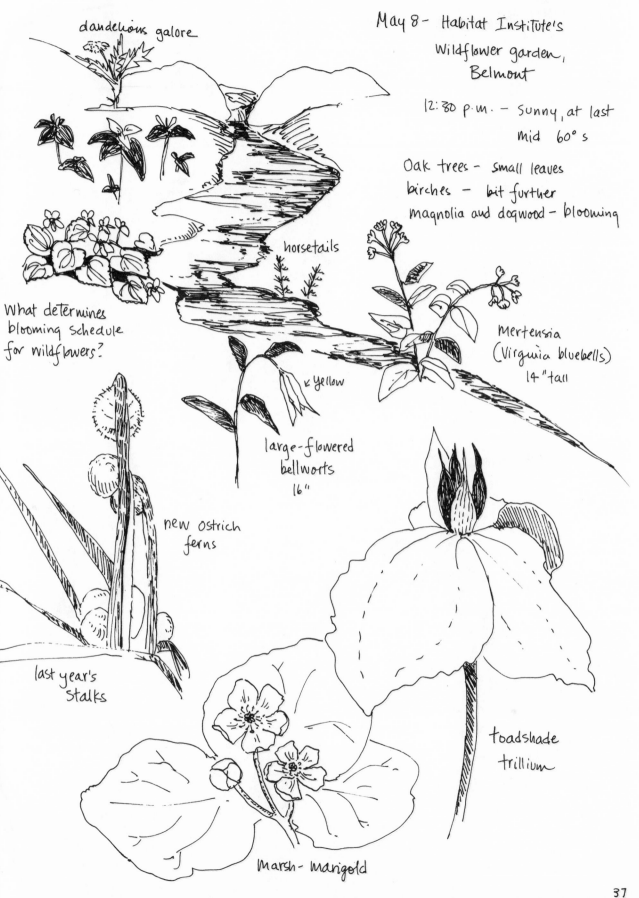

dandelions galore

May 8 - Habitat Institute's
Wildflower garden,
Belmont

12:30 p.m. - sunny, at last
Mid 60°s

Oak trees - small leaves
birches - bit further
magnolia and dogwood - blooming

horsetails

What determines
blooming schedule
for wildflowers?

Mertensia
(Virginia bluebells)
14" tall

← yellow

large-flowered
bellworts
16"

new ostrich
ferns

last year's
stalks

toadshade
trillium

Marsh-Marigold

May 12 - Mount Auburn Cemetery,
Cambridge

1:30 p.m., low 70's
humid and overcast

Driving down Brattle St.
past a fairyland of
blossoms, new leaves,
and dazzling colors.

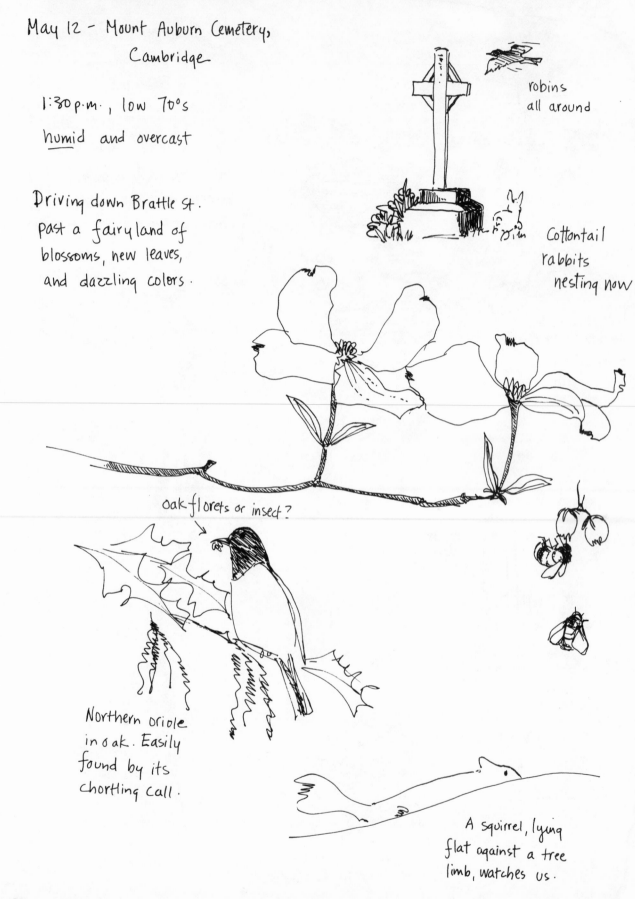

robins
all around

Cottontail
rabbits
nesting now

oak-florets or insect?

Northern oriole
in oak. Easily
found by its
chortling call.

A squirrel, lying
flat against a tree
limb, watches us.

Male towhee
scratching
about among dried
oak leaves.

Air is full of
sweet perfumed
smells.

Robin pulling up grasses
for a nest.

"weetchy - weetchy - weetchy"

Common Yellowthroat
only eight feet away.

old
← terminal bud scales

← This year's growth

American beech
leaves unfolding
along vein lines

delicately
soft
leaves

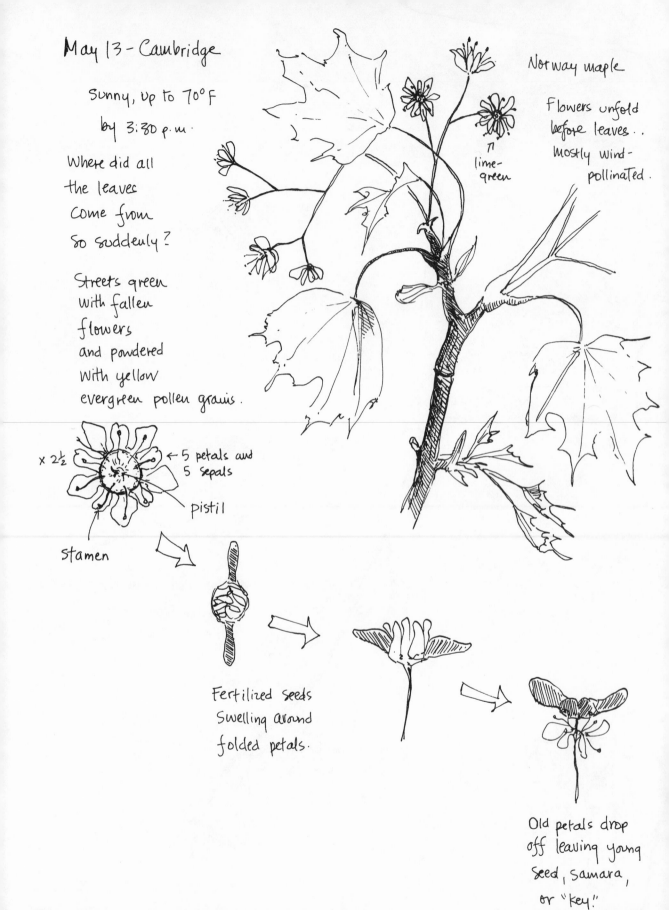

May 13 - Cambridge

Sunny, up to 70°F
by 3:30 p.m.

Where did all
the leaves
come from
so suddenly?

Streets green
with fallen
flowers
and powdered
with yellow
evergreen pollen grains.

Norway maple

Flowers unfold
before leaves..
mostly wind-
pollinated.

π
lime-
green

× 2½

← 5 petals and
5 sepals

→ pistil

Stamen

Fertilized seeds
swelling around
folded petals.

Old petals drop
off leaving young
seed, samara,
or "key!"

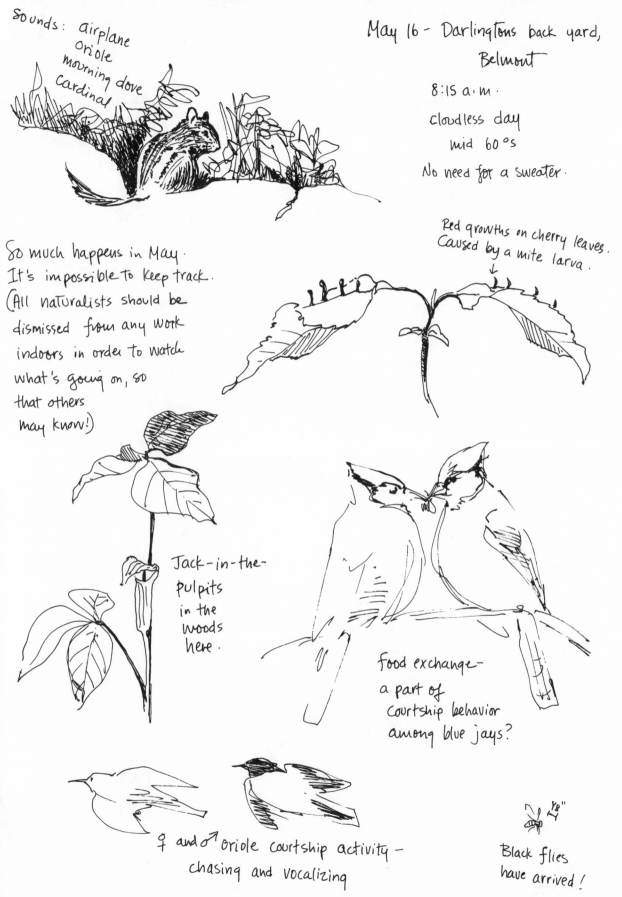

Sounds: airplane
oriole
mourning dove
Cardinal

May 16 - Darlingtons back yard,
Belmont

8:15 a.m.

cloudless day
mid 60°s
No need for a sweater.

So much happens in May.
It's impossible to keep track.
(All naturalists should be
dismissed from any work
indoors in order to watch
what's going on, so
that others
may know!)

Red growths on cherry leaves.
Caused by a mite larva.

Jack-in-the-
pulpits
in the
woods
here.

Food exchange -
a part of
courtship behavior
among blue jays?

♀ and ♂ oriole courtship activity -
chasing and vocalizing

Black flies
have arrived!

41

May 27 - Vermont

A fully spring weekend

4:30 a.m. dawn chorus
of birds in full courtship
activity

Sun sets over western
ridge about 8:05 p.m.

Sultry 85°F
at 1:30 p.m.

Black flies
pestering us all

While planting the vegetable garden, saw:

tree Swallows

goldfinch

robins

Chestnut-sided
Warbler singing
in young aspens.

Yellow-shafted
flicker

Chickadee pulling tufts
from our doormat - for a nest?

Harpo feels
the heat. —

So hard to return
to Cambridge, now.
Everything is so
bursting with activity. It's
hard to remember how
recently all was
colored black, white,
or brown and quiet.

June beetles cling to the
porch screens at night -
"bzz. bzzz" — thud-bang

10:30 a.m., low 70°s and sunny

Dusk doesn't come until 8:30 p.m.

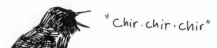

"Chir·chir·chir"

In the street outside our building, a young starling chases parent for food. (Already the size of adult.)

June is roses month!

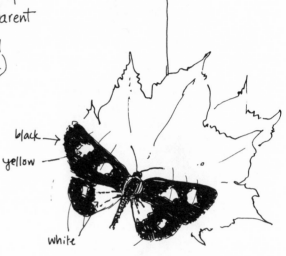

black →
yellow →

white

In Harvard Yard, an eight-spotted forester moth hovered around the ivy covering a dorm. A flashy spot of activity made me stop to watch.

Apparently these moths are abundant there in spring as they lay their eggs on the leaves. The hatched caterpillars feed on the leaves. Someone has called these the "Harvard Yard moths."

1:30 p.m.
As we turned onto Rte 93 North, a black-crowned night heron flew over.

Must have come from the Mystic River marsh to the right.

In the most unlikely places, wild things can be found.

June 10 - On top of the drumlin
Mass. Audubon Society, Lincoln
1:15 p.m.; Sunny, bit Windy

mourning dove

Fields are packed with
insect activity which
all lasts such a brief time.

Tent caterpillars
on
young cherry

Black Swallowtails
have emerged.

Dewberry
in flower,
spreading
over grasses.

fold wings
back

Skipper
on vetch

1"

Pale green and
white cocoon
of tent caterpillar
amongst
grasses.

Dark brown chrysalis
inside.

3/4"

Blue
damsel-
fly
Shimmers
in the
light.

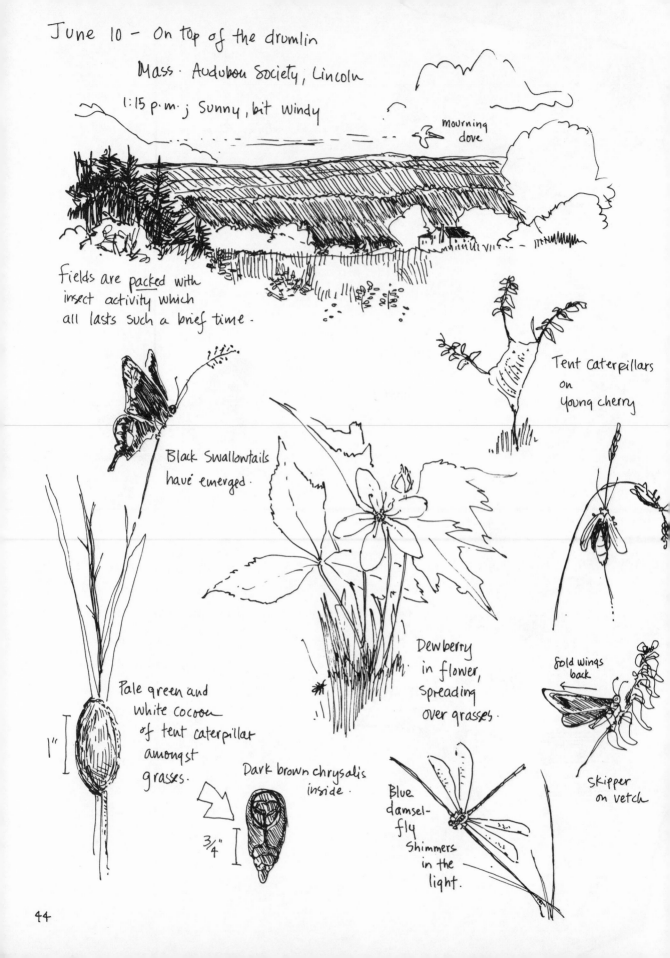

Two deer in road
when we came
last night

also a

brown hare

and a

young porcupine

June 12 – Vermont

Fireflies now out.

So quiet after Cambridge,
even though peepers, toads,
and frogs sound off through
most of night.

Everything green and
lush now. Leaves fully out
and grasses getting high.
Abundance of black flies
and mosquitoes, hence
the number of birds
around. Much calling
and bustling about
all day.

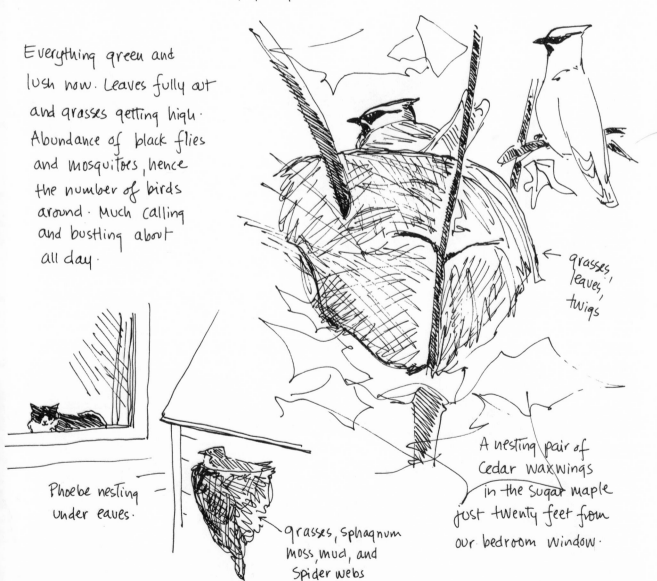

← grasses,
leaves,
twigs

Phoebe nesting
under eaves.

grasses, sphagnum
moss, mud, and
spider webs

A nesting pair of
cedar waxwings
in the sugar maple
just twenty feet from
our bedroom window.

June 19 - Vermont

Phoebe Watching

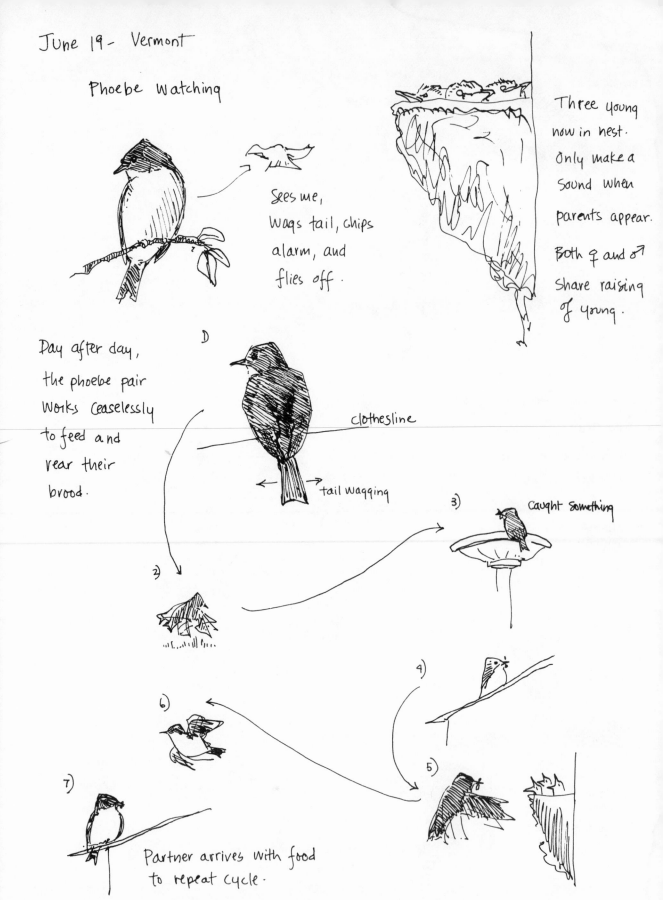

Sees me, wags tail, chips alarm, and flies off.

Three young now in nest. Only make a sound when parents appear.

Both ♀ and ♂ share raising of young.

Day after day, the phoebe pair works ceaselessly to feed and rear their brood.

D

clothesline

← →tail wagging

3) Caught something

2)

4)

6)

5)

7)

Partner arrives with food to repeat cycle.

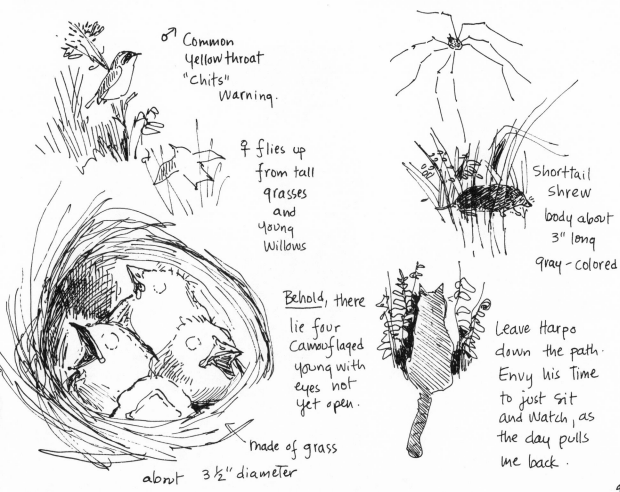

Birds are
seen now only
as shadows
darting through
leaves. Recognized
by their calls mostly.

June 20 – Vermont

8:15 a.m.

Walk down our ski
path, through birch-
maple woods.

Everything green and
twinkling in the pale
morning light

Bent down to draw a
daddy-long-legs and
a tiny shrew scuttled
close by.

♂ Common
Yellowthroat
"Chits"
Warning.

♀ flies up
from tall
grasses
and
young
Willows

Shorttail
Shrew
body about
3" long
gray-colored

Behold, there
lie four
camouflaged
young with
eyes not
yet open.

Leave Harpo
down the path.
Envy his Time
to just sit
and watch, as
the day pulls
me back.

made of grass
about 3½" diameter

First day of Summer
and the longest day.
Still light at 9:10 p.m.
while we eat on the porch.

Calls heard at
dusk:
woodcock
veery
Song Sparrow
red-eyed vireo
white-throated sparrow
red-winged blackbird
common yellowthroat
robin
ovenbird

♂ redwing:

"ook-a-lee"

Evening cools the day.
It is so peaceful here.

Woodchuck scampering
into grasses.

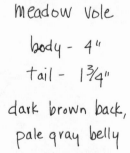

meadow vole

body - 4"

tail - 1¾"

dark brown back,
pale gray belly

Harpo brought up
onto the porch.

Flowers blooming in the
Meadows

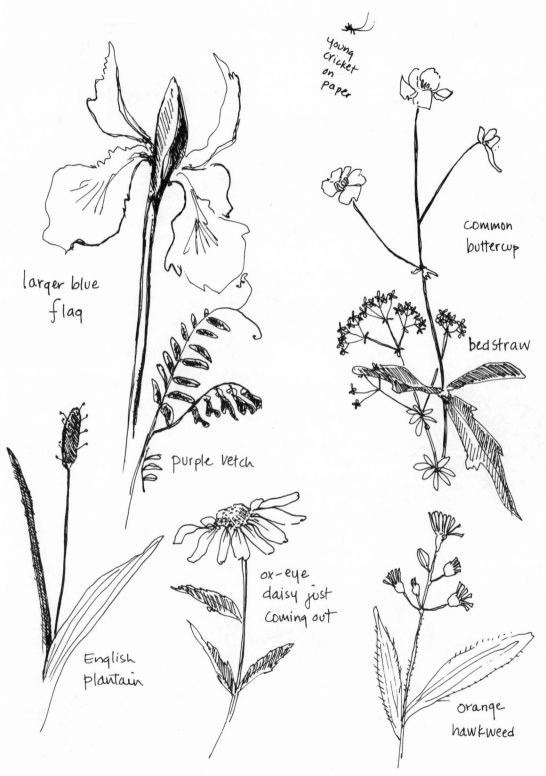

young
Cricket
on
Paper

larger blue
flag

common
buttercup

bedstraw

purple vetch

English
plantain

ox-eye
daisy just
coming out

orange
hawkweed

June 28 – Mount Auburn Cemetery,
Cambridge

6:45 p.m.

In the 90°s today and
uncomfortably humid.

For relief, took Eric
to an urban Eden of
quiet and green lushness.
(EveryTime, I say I
must come here more often!)

Saw a muskrat
at Willow Pond.
Swam away with
grasses in its mouth –
for food
or nesting?

ear tufts still

← pulsing
throat
"groonk"
"gruunk"

Then a young one appeared
from the rushes to follow after.

young squirrels

Eric in same
position as
green frog!

Sounds: traffic
airplane
goldfinch
starlings

50

Already midsummer is here.
The land is at its height of
growth and lushness.

Everything seems full of
purpose and activity.
These are healthy days.

July 5 - Vermont

Finally settled here
for the summer.

Sunrise: 5:16 a.m.
Sunset: 8:24 p.m.

Constant chatter of swallows,
grasshoppers, and crickets.
Smell of hot sun on
drying hay.

Stanley Hubbard's barn

July 7 - Vermont
Local reptiles and amphibians:

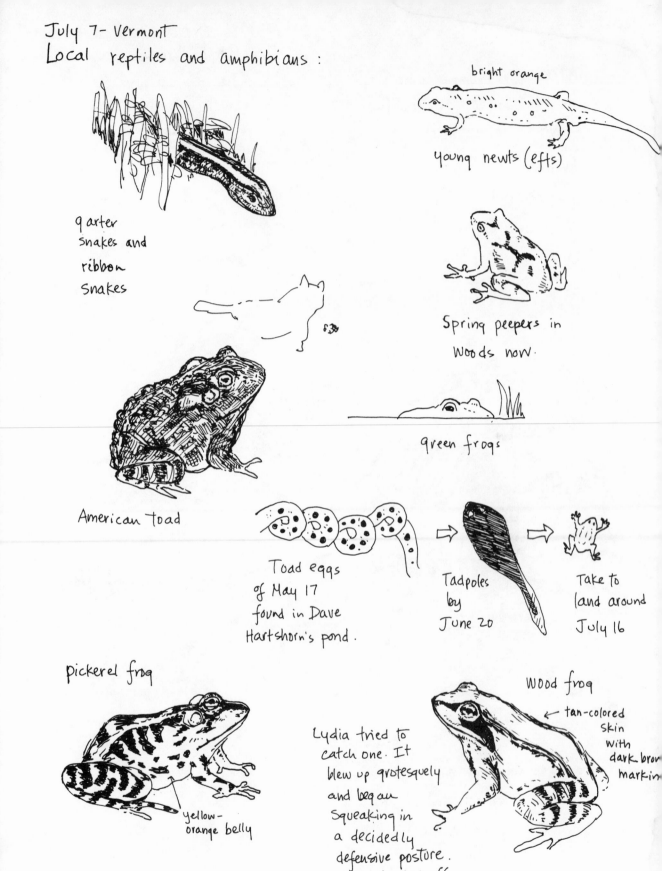

garter
snakes and
ribbon
snakes

bright orange

young newts (efts)

Spring peepers in
woods now.

green frogs

American toad

Toad eggs
of May 17
found in Dave
Hartshorn's pond.

Tadpoles
by
June 20

Take to
land around
July 16

pickerel frog

yellow-
orange belly

Lydia tried to
catch one. It
blew up grotesquely
and began
squeaking in
a decidedly
defensive posture.
Lydia backed off.

Wood frog

← tan-colored
skin
with
dark brown
marking

Porcupine at the porch door
      at 11:40 p.m.

 "gnaw - gnaw - gnaw"

(Chews the boards that
  have salt from our
  winter boots.)

Turning tail
and raising
quills.
Much teeth
chattering.
Moves
very
clumsily.

Must have been
a young 'un
because, besides
being small, it
seemed to have no
fear. It wouldn't
budge. David had
to nudge it off the
porch with a fire
poker. Little fellow
pitched into my
clematis with
much scuffling
about.

(Does have such an
odd look. As if it
had just come from
the hair dryer.)

Finally waddled slowly
into the night.

53

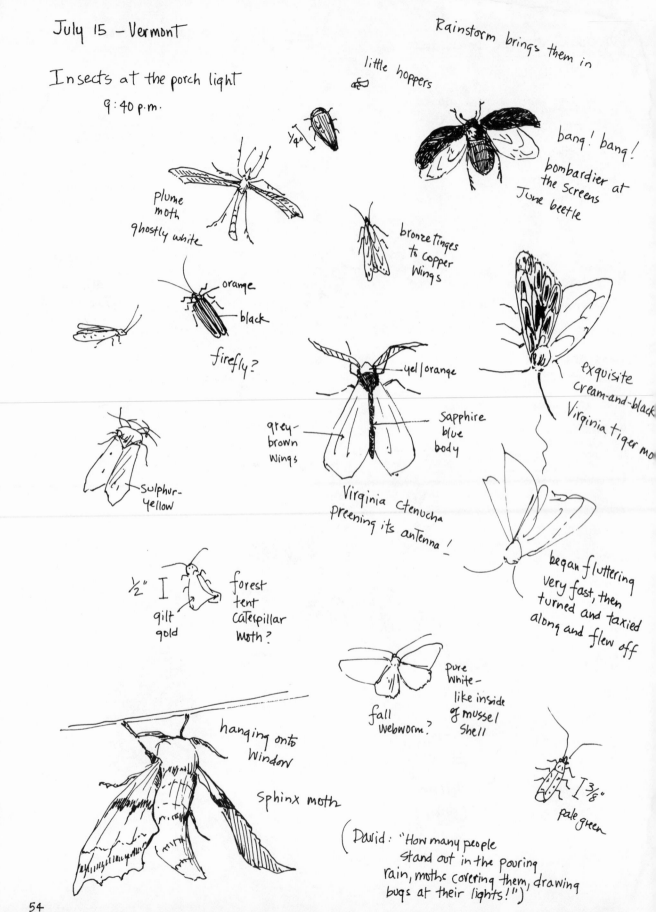

July 15 – Vermont

Insects at the porch light
9:40 p.m.

Rainstorm brings them in

little hoppers

¼"

plume
moth
ghostly white

bronze tinges
to copper
wings

bang! bang!
bombardier at
the screens
June beetle

orange

black

firefly?

yel/orange

exquisite
cream-and-black
Virginia tiger mo

grey-
brown
wings

sapphire
blue
body

sulphur-
yellow

Virginia Ctenucha
preening its antenna!

began fluttering
very fast, then
turned and taxied
along and flew off

½" I

gilt
gold

forest
tent
caterpillar
moth?

pure
white –
like inside
of mussel
shell

fall
webworm?

hanging onto
window

Sphinx moth

I ⅜"

pale green

(David: "How many people
stand out in the pouring
rain, moths covering them, drawing
bugs at their lights!")

July 20 – Vermont
5:20 p.m.

As I was jogging down our road, found a swallowtail pair locked together. Female had lost a wing and male seemed mostly crushed. She was trying to drag him along.

Death is so commonplace in nature, and so often brutal, too. Yet the urge to survive and procreate overcomes it all.

July 21
2:15 p.m.

Sitting up by the well for a moment alone in quiet. Listening to insects humming and letting the sun bake into me. A hawk circles over the ridge.

Watched a small, white butterfly caught by Sundew. The struggle did not last long as the plant closed in over it.

July 22 – Vermont

4:15 p.m.

This did happen:

1)

I saw Harpo
watching something
in our north meadow.
He often sits watching
for mice.

2)

No- Harpo had
attracted the
curiosity of a
young deer!

4)

3)

And the deer, having
lost a playmate, went
in pursuit of Harpo,
who vanished behind
the barn.

After five minutes,
the tension was too much
for Harpo. The deer flicked its
tail and off went the cat!

Long walk with Eric down our
road as evening sets in at almost 7 p.m.

hot, sunny, blue-sky day
temp. in the 80°s

That's all we saw of the beaver
in our marsh.

Lydia's
Kittens due
any day

A ruffed grouse scuttled low
across the road leaving <u>ten</u>
chicks rustling into hiding
in the spruce thickets.

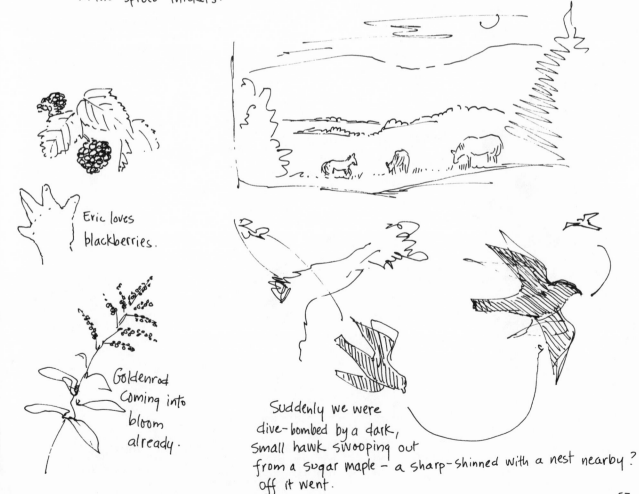

Eric loves
blackberries.

Goldenrod
coming into
bloom
already.

Suddenly we were
dive-bombed by a dark,
small hawk swooping out
from a sugar maple – a sharp-shinned with a nest nearby?
off it went.

August 1 - Vermont

Found a little brown bat disheveled in a heap on our barn floor. How had it died?

Little brown bat
Myotis lucifugus

body = 2"
Wingspread = 7½"

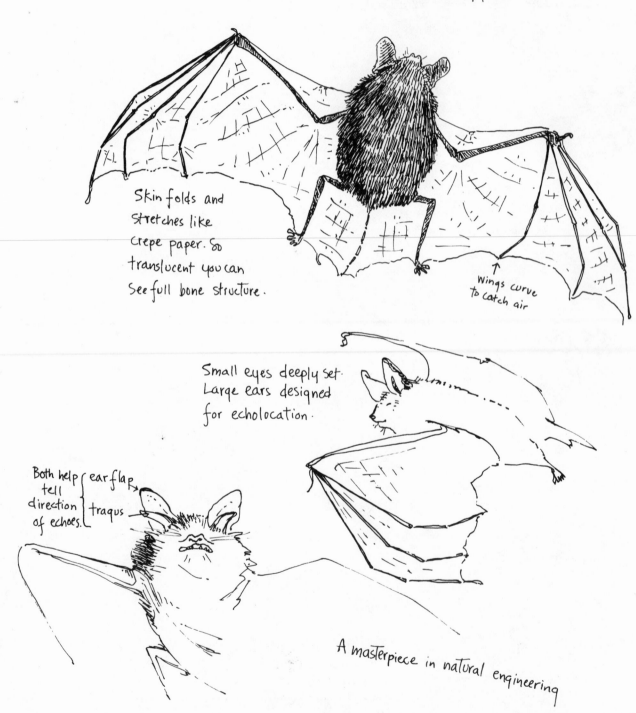

Skin folds and stretches like crepe paper. So translucent you can see full bone structure.

Wings curve to catch air

Small eyes deeply set. Large ears designed for echolocation.

Both help tell direction of echoes. { ear flap, tragus }

A masterpiece in natural engineering

Some common mosses and lichens from our land

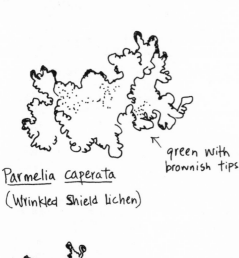

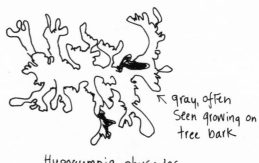

Parmelia caperata
(Wrinkled Shield Lichen)

← green with brownish tips

← gray, often seen growing on tree bark

Hypogymnia physodes
(Puffed Shield Lichen)

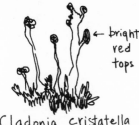

← bright red tops

Cladonia cristatella
(British Soldiers)

← pale green

Cladonia conista
(Pixie Cup)

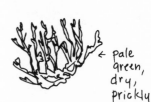

← pale green, dry, prickly

Cladonia rangiferina
(Reindeer Lichen)

Cladonia chlorophaea
(Mealy Goblet Lichen)

Cladonia degenerans
(Frayed Lichen)

Hylocomium splendens
(Mountain fern Moss)

Polytrichum commune
(Common Hairy Cap Moss)

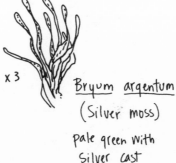

x 3

Bryum argentum
(Silver moss)

pale green with silver cast

Leucobryum glaucum
(Cushion Moss)

August 3 - Vermont

Found a field cricket on the road by Stanley's barn.

When I went to catch her, she would hop about two feet and do an almost 360° twist around in that spot and then repeat as I followed.

Finally I caught her and took her home to watch. (Let her go later that day.)

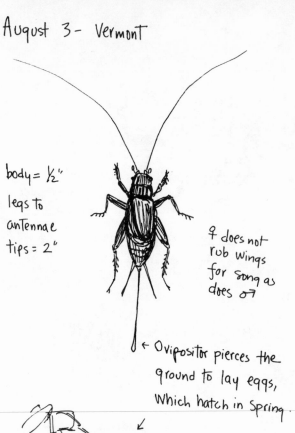

body = ½"
legs to antennae tips = 2"

♀ does not rub wings for song as does ♂

← Ovipositor pierces the ground to lay eggs, which hatch in spring.

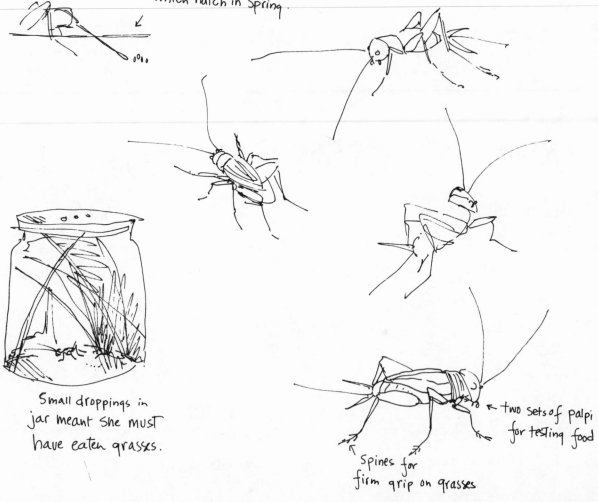

Small droppings in jar meant she must have eaten grasses.

← two sets of palpi for testing food

Spines for firm grip on grasses

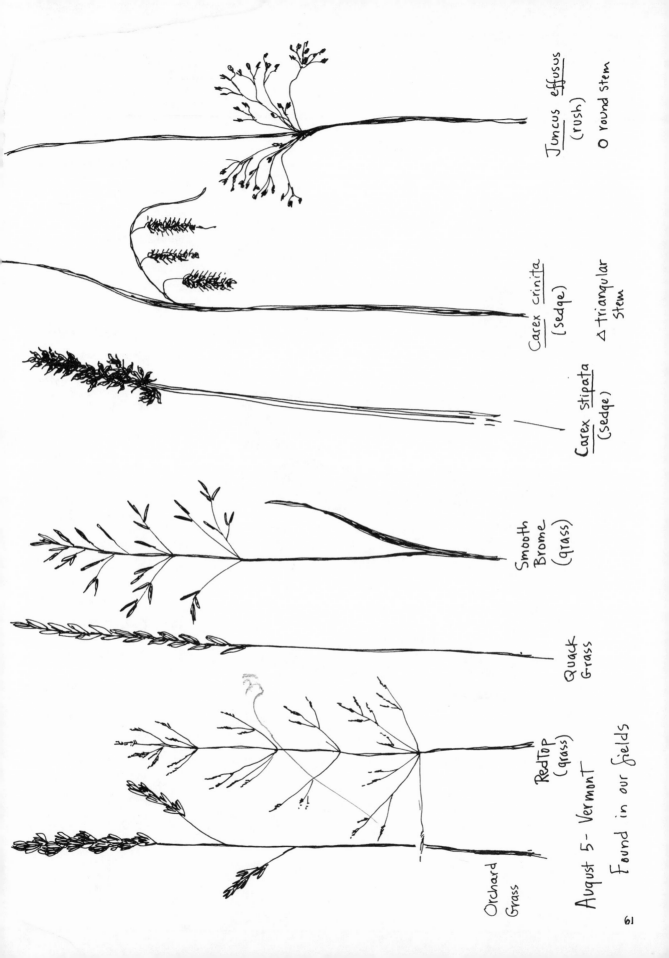

Juncus effusus
(rush)

O round stem

Carex crinita
(sedge)

△ triangular stem

Carex stipata
(Sedge)

Smooth Brome
(grass)

Quack Grass

RedTop
(grass)

Orchard Grass

August 5 - Vermont

Found in our fields

61

When I went to make Morning coffee, our stove began shooting sparks and then went off.

Upon opening up the back of the stove, we discovered a fully stocked mouse pantry!

Contents:

1. peanut shells
2. poppy seed heads
3. wishbone of last Thanksgiving's turkey
4. Brillo pads
5. tinfoil
6. iris seed heads
7. several dog biscuits
8. prune and cherry pits
9. shredded tea bags
10. nibbled flies
11. birdseed
12. insulation fluff
13. barberry seeds
14. and, charred mouse fur and nibbled wires

Some local residents:

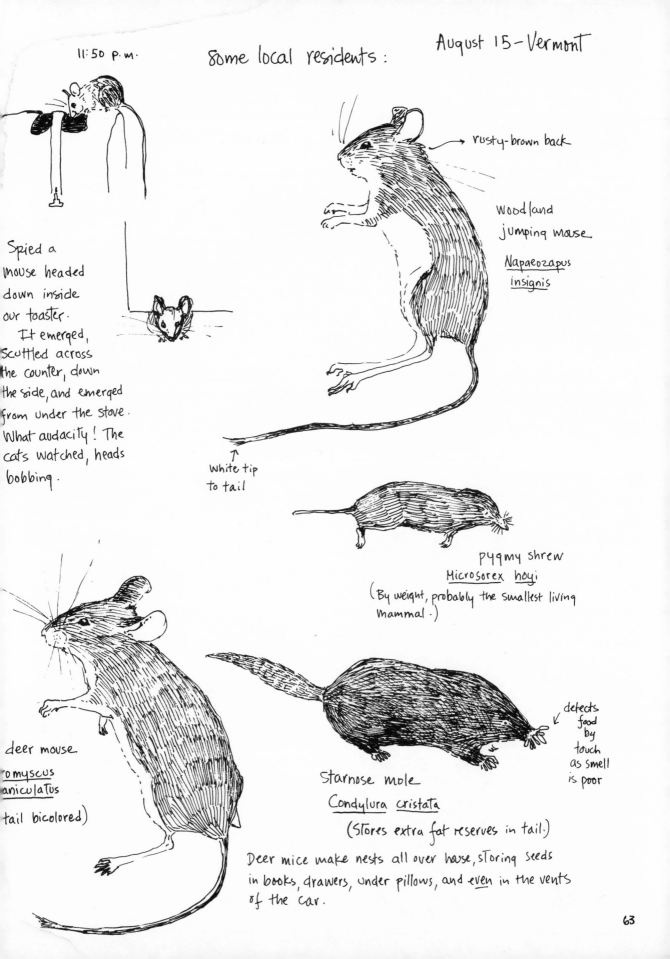

→ rusty-brown back

Woodland
jumping mouse

Napaeozapus
insignis

Spied a
mouse headed
down inside
our toaster.

It emerged,
scuttled across
the counter, down
the side, and emerged
from under the stove.
What audacity! The
cats watched, heads
bobbing.

↑
white tip
to tail

Pygmy shrew
Microsorex hoyi
(By weight, probably the smallest living
mammal.)

deer mouse
Peromyscus
maniculatus

(tail bicolored)

Starnose mole
Condylura cristata

(Stores extra fat reserves in tail.)

← detects
food
by
touch
as smell
is poor

Deer mice make nests all over house, storing seeds
in books, drawers, under pillows, and even in the vents
of the car.

August 23

Afternoon before, she had tried hopping through the porch railing. (We think this started her contractions.)

On our bed, David and I watch:

3:35 a.m: A suspicious "meeoouw!"

3:45 a.m.
She yowls and pushes and out comes a wet, wiggling live kitten!
It is amazing how instinct takes control.

about 3"
more like a small rat

Minutes old, and already it is nursing and mewing.

Up against her tail, no mess on our bed under the towel, no odor. She is already producing #2!

She eats the birth sac* and bites off the umbilical cord.
4:30 a.m.

* Placenta has a lot of energy-giving nutrients in it.

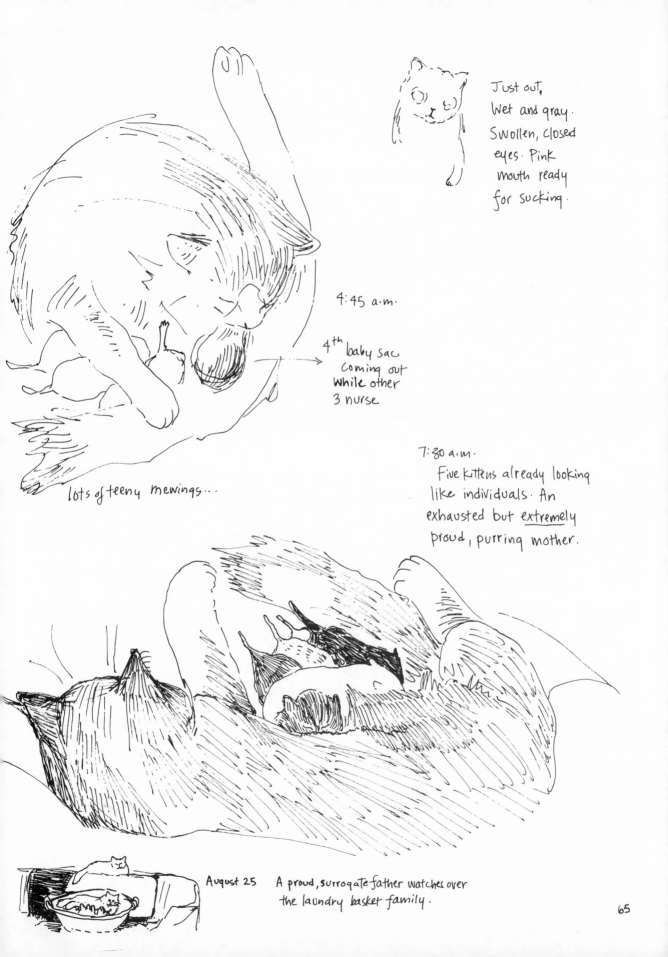

Just out,
Wet and gray.
Swollen, closed
eyes. Pink
mouth ready
for sucking.

4:45 a.m.

4th baby sac
coming out
while other
3 nurse

lots of teeny mewings...

7:30 a.m.
Five kittens already looking
like individuals. An
exhausted but _extremely_
proud, purring mother.

August 25   A proud, surrogate father watches over
the laundry basket family.

65

August 26 -   Vermont
    9:40 p.m.   56°F

The black sky is thick
  with stars. A distant
  coyote barks.

Things have slowed their
  hectic pace of growth.
  August is a moment
  of rest, of quiet, before
  activity resumes for
  the winter preparations.

Scorpio

SW
over
red pines

Cassiopeia

NE over
the house

7:30 p.m. - sunset
6:10 a.m. - sunrise

Days now noticeably
  shorter.

vegetable
garden

South view

goldenrod
purple- and white-flowered
    asters
drying ferns and grasses
maturing milkweed pods
black-eyed Susan

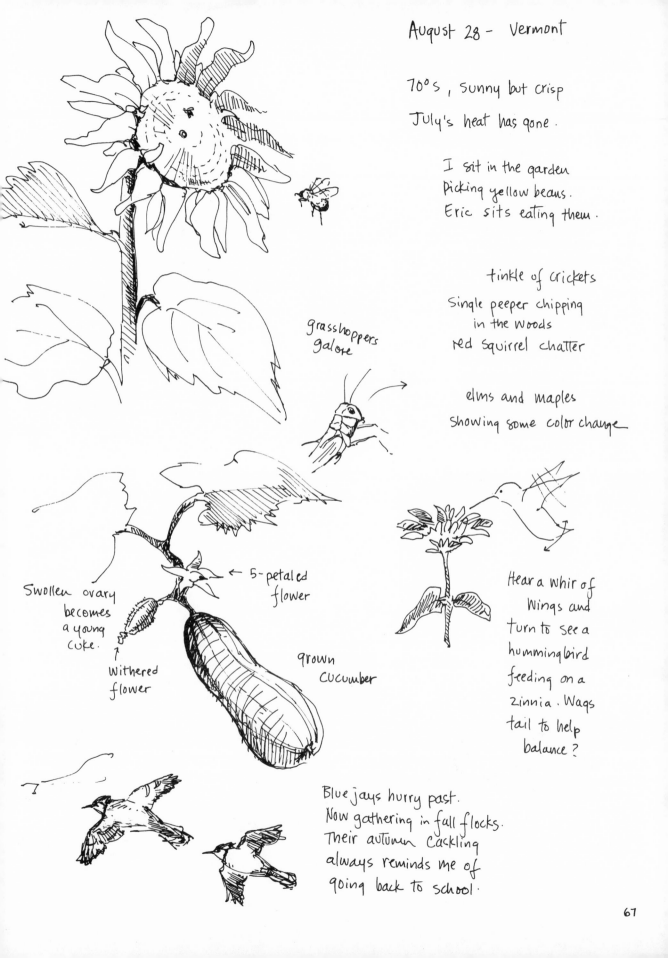

August 28 - Vermont

70's, sunny but crisp
July's heat has gone.

I sit in the garden
picking yellow beans.
Eric sits eating them.

tinkle of crickets
Single peeper chipping
in the woods
red squirrel chatter

elms and maples
showing some color change

grasshoppers
galore

5-petaled
flower

Swollen ovary
becomes
a young
cuke.

Withered
flower

grown
Cucumber

Hear a whir of
wings and
turn to see a
hummingbird
feeding on a
zinnia. Wags
tail to help
balance?

Bluejays hurry past.
Now gathering in fall flocks.
Their autumn Cackling
always reminds me of
going back to school.

September 10 – Cambridge

low 80°s   – oppressively muggy

How different a cricket sounds chirping in Cambridge!

Heard a chickadee's "phee-be" song outside my window.
   Even though it was a common sound in Vermont all summer,
   I was keenly aware of it here.

Cambridge is a box of humanity. In it, one's orientation is
toward people and people's needs. Nature feels ~~~> OUT THERE.

But, oh the joy of finding wild things in unexpected places: a
female cricket chirping and jumping about in our basement; a garden
spider crossing the sidewalk; a mockingbird in a neighbor's crab apple;
and even the pigeons bowing and posturing at each other on
Cambridge Common.

   But, after a summer of open spaces and country silence, and
living surrounded by wild things, the change takes some getting
used to.

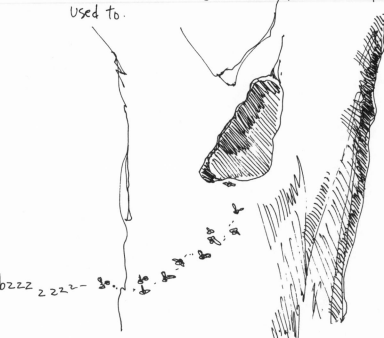

The first honey bee
tree I've seen –
   and right here
   on Oxford St!

bzzz z zz² –

Weeds Next Door

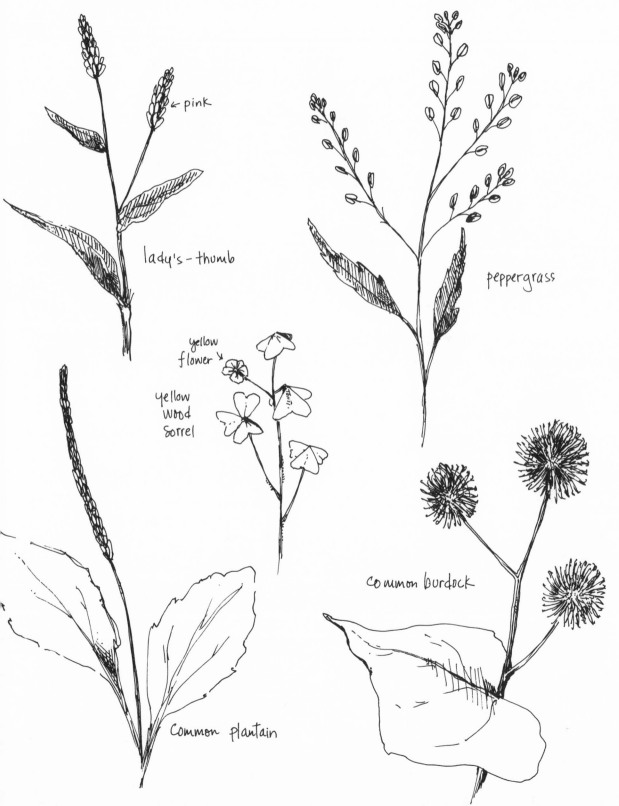

← pink

lady's-thumb

peppergrass

yellow
flower ↘

Yellow
Wood
Sorrel

Common plantain

Common burdock

September 15 - McLean Hospital's land,
                    Belmont

2:15 p.m.

Sunny, high 70's

Such a tangle of
growth since last
I came here.
   Already plants
dying back, leaves
fading, seeds dispersed,
nests abandoned

Lots of grasshopper zips
and cricket chirps

Crows
Calling

Goldenrod
and
asters in
bloom

redtop grasses

cricket

Sumac
with red
fruits

Milkweed
pods not
yet open

Poison ivy
leaves
turning
red

(I remember so well
walking these woods
and fields with Marie Henry,
who died much too soon.)

ctenucha
moth

hornet

ant

black and
yellow

locust borer
beetle

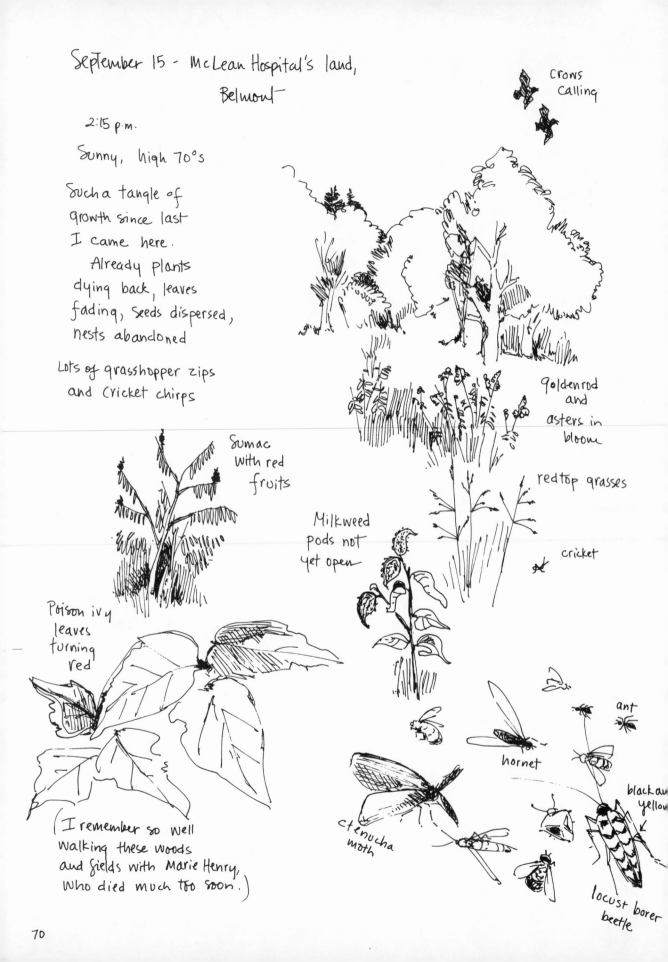

September 19 - Vermont

Heard first a
high-pitched
"Keee
eeer"

Back in Cambridge;
we catch only weekend
glimpses of Vermont.

The ridges are beginning
to turn scarlet and yellow.

A light-phase
red-tailed hawk flew
over the garden
while I pulled
up last of
carrots and
beets.

Kittens playing all
day beside the wood
stove, which now goes
all the time.

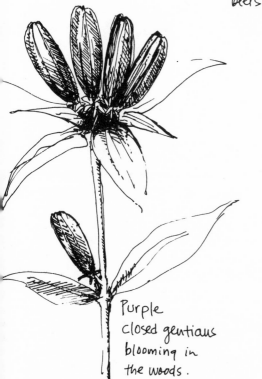

Purple
closed gentians
blooming in
the woods.

A chipmunk darted into a
hole in base of sugar maple
on the front lawn. Turned to eye
me and some of its provisions
fell down. A winter home inside?

September 26 - Cambridge

2:10 p.m.

Clearing after yesterday's
rain - Sweater weather

Dogwood berries
are eaten
by robins

Time for noticing berries
and nuts (and
their gatherers)

maple
"key"

← young
bud

linden
seeds

Squirrel
eating maple
seeds

horsechestnuts
in the streets

marigolds in
everybody's
yards

Crab apple tree full
of chattering starlings
eating its yellow fruits.

Squirrels are busily
burying acorns.

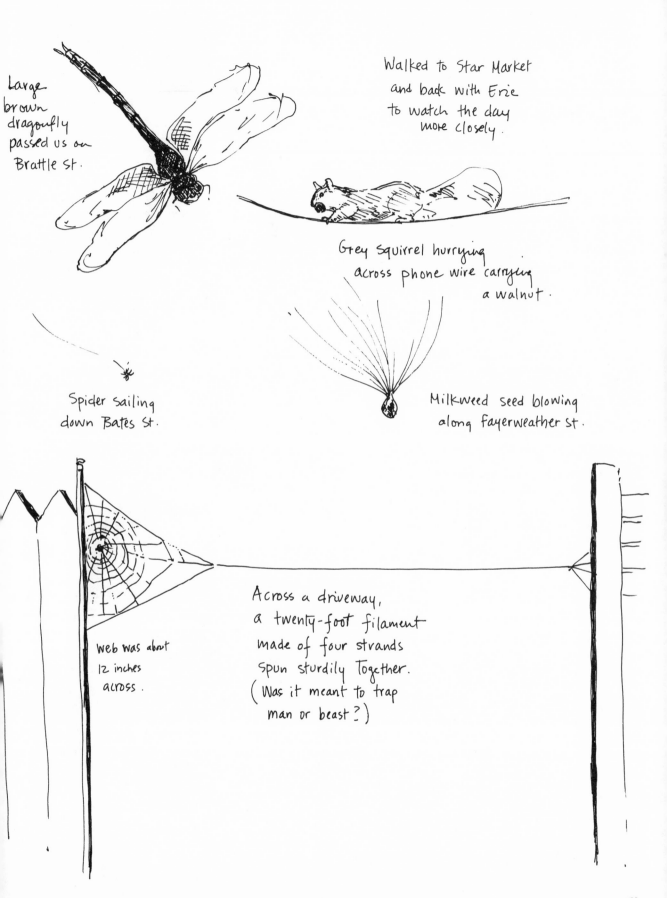

Large brown dragonfly passed us on Brattle St.

Walked to Star Market and back with Erie to watch the day more closely.

Grey squirrel hurrying across phone wire carrying a walnut.

Spider sailing down Bates St.

Milkweed seed blowing along Fayerweather St.

Web was about 12 inches across.

Across a driveway, a twenty-foot filament made of four strands spun sturdily together. (Was it meant to trap man or beast?)

Lydia brought in a
bird for her kittens.

Canada warbler

immature
or
fall plumage

slight dark
necklace

blue/gray
back and
Saffron
Yellow
breast

body = 4 ¾"

Where had this bird
Come from and where
Was it headed?

Gray and rainy. Mists
in the valleys. Fall is
truly here. Colors
have peaked. Although
the fields are still green,
leaves are off the trees on tops
of the ridges.

Insect tinkles heard
during only the warmest
parts of the day.

4:30 p.m.
Through gray
skies came a
honking wedge
of geese,
speeding south.

A single angle wing
butterfly at our
porch. An
over-wintering
adult.

Deer eyes in the
meadow

October 15 - Duxbury Beach

Sunny, crisp - light breeze
60°s

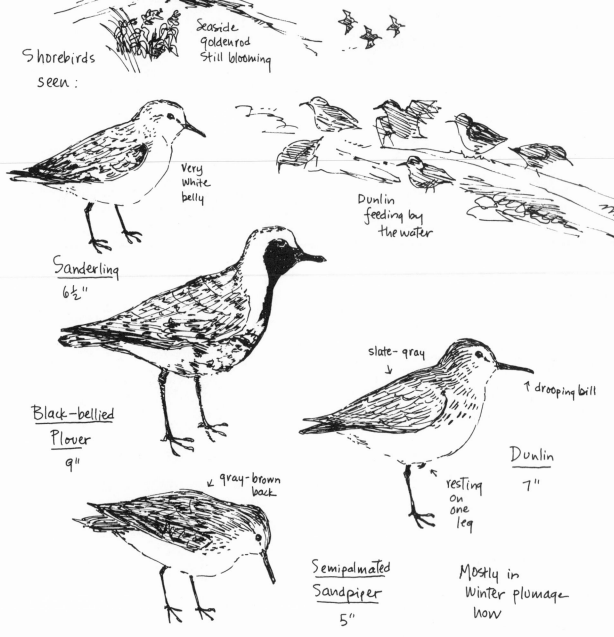

Seaside
goldenrod
still blooming

Shorebirds
seen:

Very
white
belly

Dunlin
feeding by
the water

Sanderling
6½"

Black-bellied
Plover
9"

slate-gray
↓

↑ drooping bill

Dunlin
7"

resting
on
one
leg

← gray-brown
back

Semipalmated
Sandpiper
5"

Mostly in
winter plumage
now

oranges
Soft yellows
rusts
dulling
green

Three
Shovelers

rds seen:

Green-winged teal
Wigeon
black duck
Wood duck
Mallard
American bittern
Sora rail
Song sparrow
Swamp sparrow
Shoveler
Canada geese

I find
the distractions
of the day ease
away while
watching these
magnificent
forms.

October 27 – McLean Hospital's land, Belmont

3:15 p.m. and already sun low.
Back to standard time yesterday
43° F and chilly

I feel so aware of the quick passing of time. Only yesterday these fields were just coming alive with spring activity.

Sunset by 4:45 p.m.

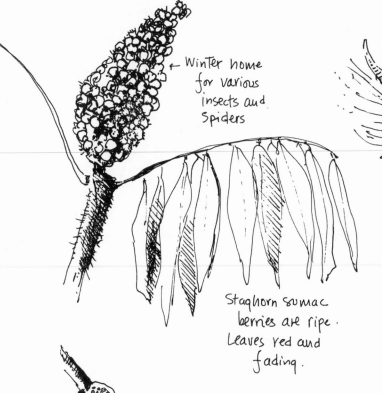

← Winter home for various insects and spiders

Staghorn sumac berries are ripe. Leaves red and fading.

Milkweed glistening in the light

Silver-shining egg cases of tent caterpillars on cherry trees. Waiting to hatch next spring.

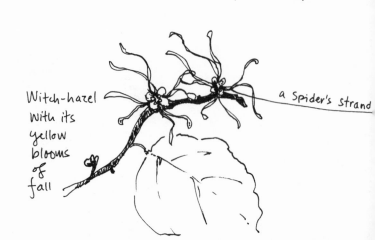

Witch-hazel with its yellow blooms of fall

a spider's strand

Small bands of
robins heartily
eating cherries
and crab apples
before heading
south. Much
clucking and
vocal interactions.

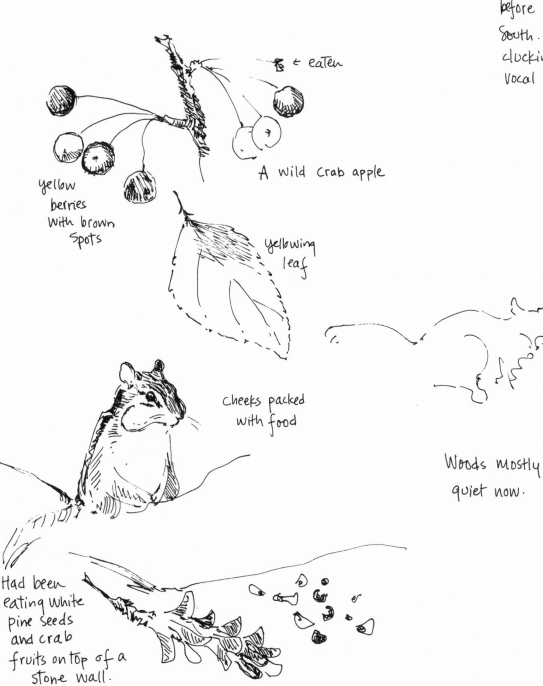

← eaten

A wild crab apple

yellow
berries
with brown
spots

Yellowing
leaf

cheeks packed
with food

Woods mostly
quiet now.

Had been
eating white
pine seeds
and crab
fruits on top of a
stone wall.

October 29 - Vermont

Dark <u>so</u> early in the
afternoon and dark
when we get up to
a cold house and
smoldering
wood stove.

Red squirrels
storing apples
in crotches
of trees for
winter eating.

Leaves off the trees.
Landscape now browns,
grays, and violets.
A few yellow tamarack
and aspen.

"bzzzz"

Cluster flies
have come into
the house (along
with the mice).

← darkened face
as camouflage

Bow-and-
arrow seas
has begun
Deer
beware.

As dusk came,
we watched two beaver
building up their lodge
for winter. A chill
came to the air
and made us
shiver.

The woods are
no longer safe
for us to walk
in, either.

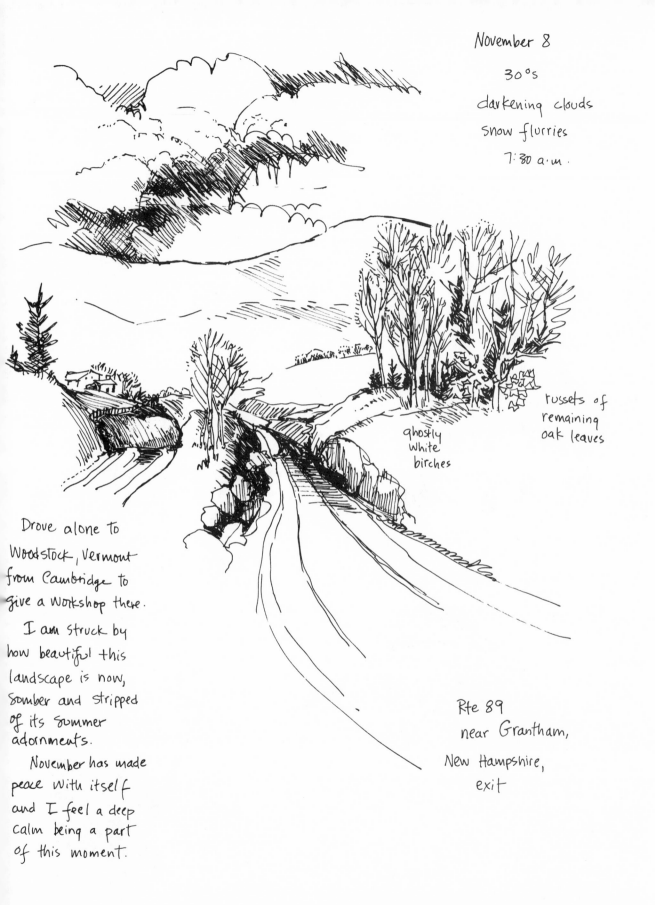

November 8
30's
darkening clouds
snow flurries
7:30 a.m.

russets of
remaining
oak leaves

ghostly
white
birches

Drove alone to
Woodstock, Vermont
from Cambridge to
give a workshop there.

I am struck by
how beautiful this
landscape is now,
somber and stripped
of its summer
adornments.

November has made
peace with itself
and I feel a deep
calm being a part
of this moment.

Rte 89
near Grantham,
New Hampshire,
exit

November 10 – Cambridge

4:30 p.m.

Walked along back
streets with Eric
in the backpack.

60's – warmish

(Fall still here, if not
in Vermont.)

(Some Norway maples
still holding yellow,
floppy leaves.)

Starlings cluster
in trees for their
evening roost.

Noticed some courtship behavior
going on among several pigeons: Wing-
clapping, bowing, and tail-dragging
by males in front of females.
(Courtship displays can be
observed throughout fall
and winter.)

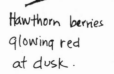

In winter, both males
and females have
a darker bill and
heavily speckled, grayer
plumage. In spring, tips of feathers
wear off to produce the bright
breeding plumage.

Hawthorn berries
glowing red
at dusk.

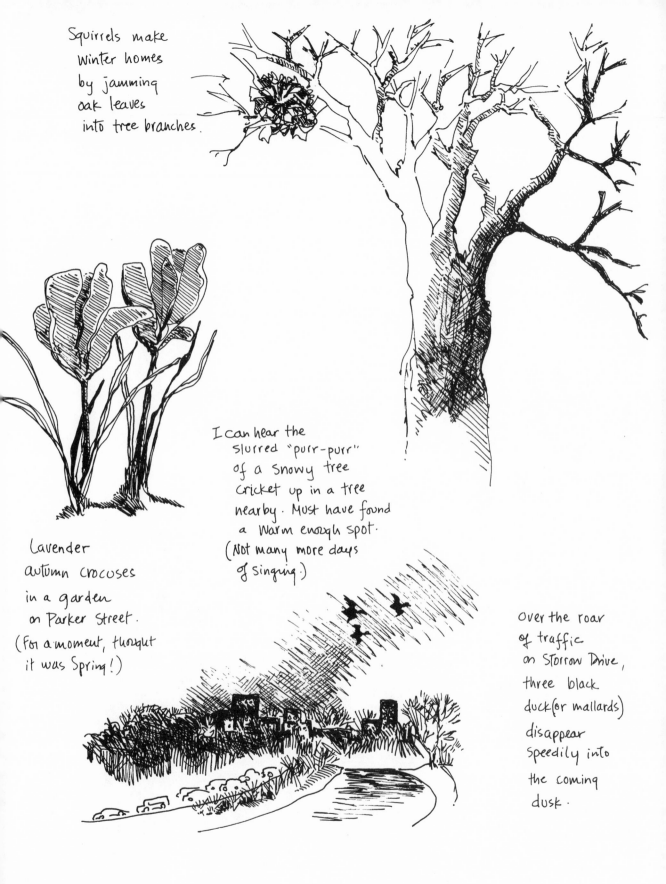

Squirrels make
winter homes
by jamming
oak leaves
into tree branches.

Lavender
autumn crocuses
in a garden
on Parker Street.
(For a moment, thought
it was Spring!)

I can hear the
slurred "purr-purr"
of a snowy tree
cricket up in a tree
nearby. Must have found
a warm enough spot.
(Not many more days
of singing.)

Over the roar
of traffic
on Storrow Drive,
three black
duck (or mallards)
disappear
speedily into
the coming
dusk.

83

November 15 – Vermont – first day of hunting season

　　　　low 30's

6:15 a.m. – up with Eric

Still dark but four trucks already in our driveway.

Many deer in our area, as the woods are still somewhat open, browsing is good, and there are numerous apple trees and young saplings.

Hunters decorate the brown landscape with their bright orange and red plaid gear

November is mating
season when deer are in
their best health and at
their most evident.

Antlers are used by
males in courtship
battles and drop off
in late winter. Size
of antlers is determined
by nutrition as
well as age.

Coat changes
from summer's
rust to gray
in winter and
has denser,
longer hair.

Hunting season coincides
with the most active
and healthiest time
of year for deer.

3/4" deer
dropping

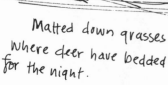

Matted down grasses
where deer have bedded
for the night.

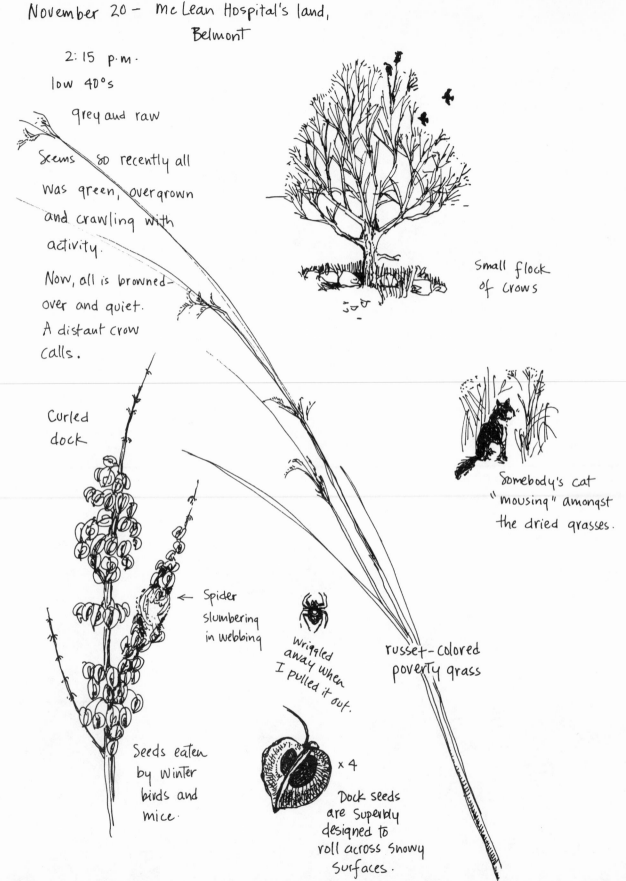

November 20 — McLean Hospital's land,
Belmont

2:15 p.m.

low 40's

grey and raw

Seems so recently all
was green, overgrown
and crawling with
activity.

Now, all is browned-
over and quiet.
A distant crow
calls.

Small flock
of crows

Curled
dock

Somebody's cat
"mousing" amongst
the dried grasses.

← Spider
slumbering
in webbing

Wriggled
away when
I pulled it out.

russet-colored
poverty grass

Seeds eaten
by winter
birds and
mice.

× 4

Dock seeds
are superbly
designed to
roll across snowy
surfaces.

November 30- Vermont

Thanksgiving weekend

Last of hunting season.
We have not been able
to walk in the woods
for three weeks.

Three days of rain, sleet,
snow, ice, rain, sleet,
snow, ice

Some days there
simply isn't anything
interesting to observe.
Drab outdoors makes
the soul drab indoors.

bzzzz

cleaning
its wings
or legs.

Eric and I
watch house flies
buzzing on our
windows.

Decided to learn about
house flies:

1. Get food with sucking proboscis since
   don't have biting mouthparts. Saliva
   dissolves substances.
2. Legs have hairs and sticky pads that
   help fly hold onto surfaces.
3. ♀ lays about 500 eggs. From egg to adult
   takes only a week. Adult lives 19-30 days.
4. Slows down activity when temperature drops
   into 40°s.

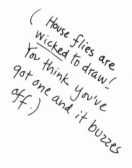

(House flies are
wicked to draw -
You think you've
got one and it buzzes
off.)

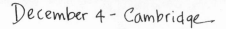

December 4 - Cambridge

   3:30 p.m. walk with Erie
through Cambridge streets.
Dusk coming on.
A scarlet sunset behind
dark, silhouetted trees.

Snowed 5" of wet,
sloppy snow last night.
Enough to close schools.

Winter seems officially here.
There is a magic to these
back streets all decked in white
and glittering with lights from
porches and cozy-looking interiors.

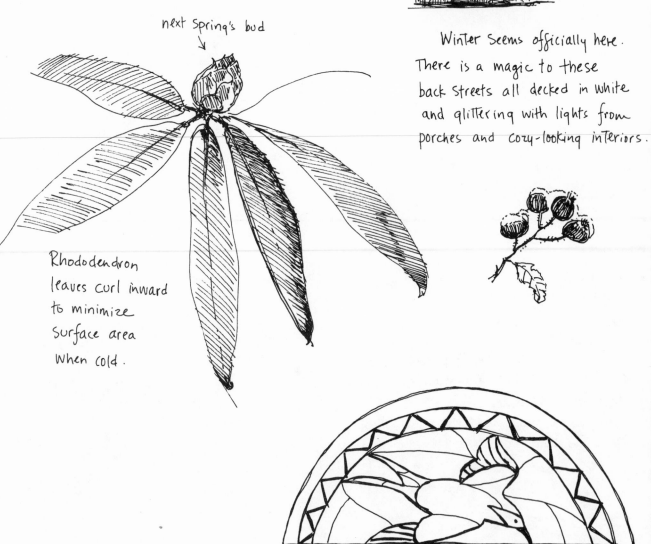

next spring's bud

Rhododendron
leaves curl inward
to minimize
surface area
when cold.

In the dark, a stained glass bird (a tern?) glows over
a doorway. The beauty of natural form strikes many people.

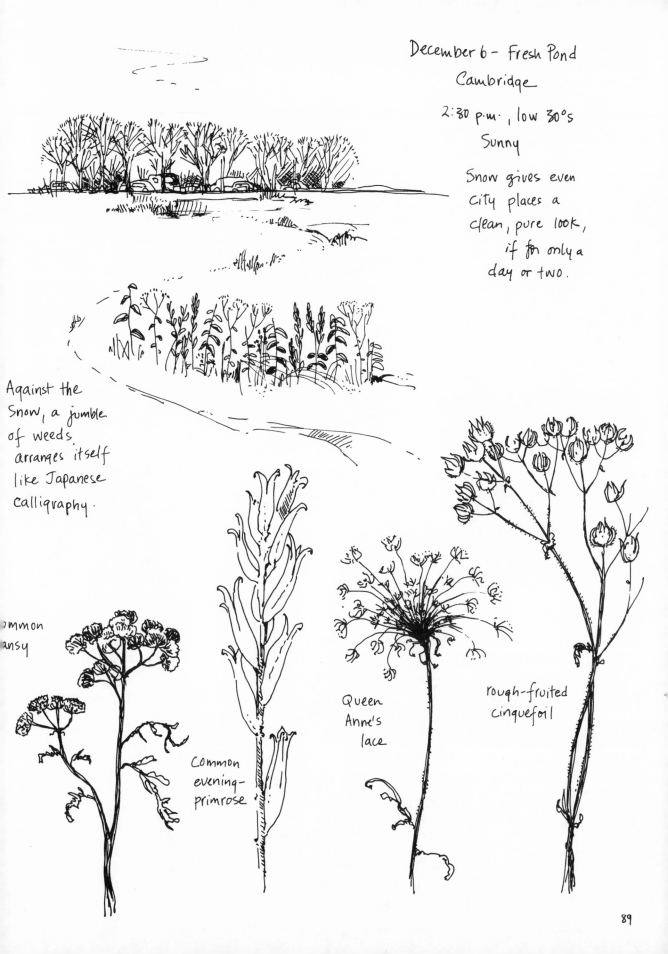

December 6 – Fresh Pond
Cambridge

2:30 p.m., low 30°s
Sunny

Snow gives even
City places a
clean, pure look,
if for only a
day or two.

Against the
Snow, a jumble
of weeds
arranges itself
like Japanese
calligraphy.

Common
tansy

Common
evening-
primrose

Queen
Anne's
lace

rough-fruited
cinquefoil

December 10 - Vermont

Arrived at 11:30 p.m.
last night. Bitter cold.
   16° F outdoors
   30° F indoors
Wonderful to hear silence
   again.
Awoke to snow blowing
past. Six inches on the
ground by afternoon.

snow formations on:

There is a different
beauty to the winter
woods from that of other
seasons. It is
subdued, simplified,
and more intimate.

balsam fir

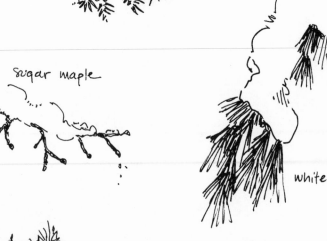
sugar maple

white pine

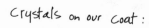
Crystals on our coat:

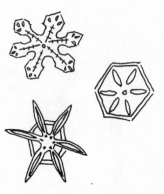

(We miss Shane's romping on
these walks. Our beloved setter
died in October.)

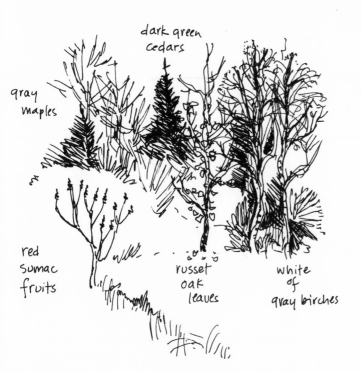

gray maples

dark green cedars

red sumac fruits

russet oak leaves

white of gray birches

December 14 - McLean Hospital's land, Belmont

2 p.m., high 30's raw and overcast no snow

On a gray day, colors stand out so remarkably.

Brilliant yellow bitternut hickory buds

Red maples have reddening buds already.

Scarlet- and-green blueberry twigs

Dazzling violet of black raspberry canes

December 20 - Vermont

Winter solstice and first day of winter

Sunrise: 7:22 a.m.

Sun went behind western ridge at 3:50 p.m.

-10°F last night

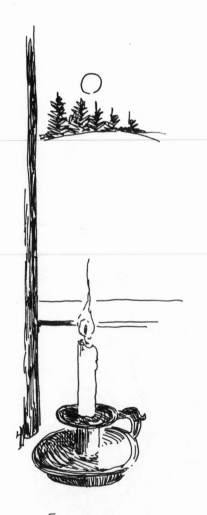

Full moon on this darkest of nights

In winter, the woods are mostly silent. An occasional cascade of snow.

Deer, hare, and porcupine tracks. Here and there a red squirrel or mouse tracing over the snow.

Winter is rest for summer's action.

A well-worn path to our barn.

December 25 - Vermont

Awoke early and
took a ski alone,
to see what
Christmas Day
was like outdoors.

deer tracks

Vole hole
in snow

Snow was glistening
in the fields.
Heard only the sound
of my skis.
A quiet time for
reflection.

December 28 – Vermont

Climbed ridge behind
our house using
snowshoes.

Climbed through predominantly
Sugar maple, paper birch and
beech woods, through red
spruce and balsam fir
to summit with
hobblebush, yellow
birch and
red maples.

Wonderful
Snow
Shadows

weasel
tracks

red spruce

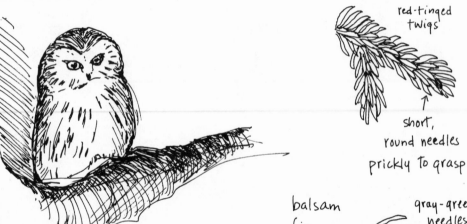

red-tinged
twigs

short,
round needles
prickly to grasp

balsam
fir

gray-green
needles

two,
white
stripes
underneath

long,
flat needles
soft to grasp

We paused To
drink some tea.
Looked up to see
a small owl
staring fixedly
down at us.
    Was a
    Saw-whet.

December 31 – Vermont

Last day of the year

From the hectic pace of Cambridge life, we too are resting here. Days consist of hauling wood, baking bread, keeping warm, and all that it takes to survive a northern winter.

View north

Now E. is almost walking.

Nesting in Eric's diapers!

Another year is passing. A new one is about to begin. The cycle continues without halt. And so, after winter will come spring.

Field Notes

January

January

February

March

April

May

June

July

August

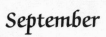
September

we all went to the marsh at about 3:00 pm. we found a deer bed but I don't think I can draw it.

Oct. 12.
beggar's tick OR I call them Vampire's fag's I was totley coverd with them. belive me! it's hurts when you walk. you

oct 12

stem

gall

this is a wasp gall wasp's lay their eggs in a stem of a plant and then the stem swells up

seeds

stem

fluf.

stem

this is a yo cat tail sort of in blum it all flues out me and leah picked some.

there's the big always bird that always a lost fly's in the bird. midst of the others.

other little bird's.

big flock of who knows what kind of bird's they are, very far away.

October

November

November

December

December